Martina-Cezara Albutiu

Scalable Analytical Query Processing

Martina-Cezara Albutiu

Scalable Analytical Query Processing

Südwestdeutscher Verlag für Hochschulschriften

Impressum / Imprint
Bibliografische Information der Deutschen Nationalbibliothek: Die Deutsche Nationalbibliothek verzeichnet diese Publikation in der Deutschen Nationalbibliografie; detaillierte bibliografische Daten sind im Internet über http://dnb.d-nb.de abrufbar.
Alle in diesem Buch genannten Marken und Produktnamen unterliegen warenzeichen-, marken- oder patentrechtlichem Schutz bzw. sind Warenzeichen oder eingetragene Warenzeichen der jeweiligen Inhaber. Die Wiedergabe von Marken, Produktnamen, Gebrauchsnamen, Handelsnamen, Warenbezeichnungen u.s.w. in diesem Werk berechtigt auch ohne besondere Kennzeichnung nicht zu der Annahme, dass solche Namen im Sinne der Warenzeichen- und Markenschutzgesetzgebung als frei zu betrachten wären und daher von jedermann benutzt werden dürften.

Bibliographic information published by the Deutsche Nationalbibliothek: The Deutsche Nationalbibliothek lists this publication in the Deutsche Nationalbibliografie; detailed bibliographic data are available in the Internet at http://dnb.d-nb.de.
Any brand names and product names mentioned in this book are subject to trademark, brand or patent protection and are trademarks or registered trademarks of their respective holders. The use of brand names, product names, common names, trade names, product descriptions etc. even without a particular marking in this works is in no way to be construed to mean that such names may be regarded as unrestricted in respect of trademark and brand protection legislation and could thus be used by anyone.

Coverbild / Cover image: www.ingimage.com

Verlag / Publisher:
Südwestdeutscher Verlag für Hochschulschriften
ist ein Imprint der / is a trademark of
OmniScriptum GmbH & Co. KG
Heinrich-Böcking-Str. 6-8, 66121 Saarbrücken, Deutschland / Germany
Email: info@svh-verlag.de

Herstellung: siehe letzte Seite /
Printed at: see last page
ISBN: 978-3-8381-3770-4

Zugl. / Approved by: München, TU, Diss., 2013

Copyright © 2013 OmniScriptum GmbH & Co. KG
Alle Rechte vorbehalten. / All rights reserved. Saarbrücken 2013

Abstract

Analytical query processing in database systems aims at providing the requested information within an acceptable response time while affecting the performance of concurrently executed transactional workloads as little as possible. Scalability in the context of analytical query processing refers to the ability of the database system to process highly data-intensive and complex queries efficiently and to take advantage of additional resources to improve query execution performance. In order to achieve the goal of scalable analytical query processing, we examine the following three approaches, which focus on response time, robustness, and resource utilization of analytical queries.

First, we investigate *synergy-based workload management* for exploiting synergies between a multitude of analytical queries which are executed concurrently. The knowledge of the synergies among queries for a given workload allows to process them in an efficient way with respect to our goals. For example, for caching synergies, by executing queries reading the same data in parallel, we minimize the buffer pool requirements as well as the I/O time of these queries. Based on the fact that both positive and negative synergies are reflected by the execution time of the workload, we develop a black box approach which flexibly adapts to any database system or hardware configuration. By monitoring and collecting the execution times of different query sets at runtime and by correlating this information, we draw conclusions regarding the synergies of queries. This information can instantly be applied by the scheduling component in order to maximize performance.

Second, we concentrate on the *robust query execution* of single database queries. In particular, we examine the join operator, a central operator in many analytical queries. Due to outdated statistics or mistaken optimizer decisions, query execution might be far from optimal and, in particular, not predictable at all in terms of both duration and resource utilization. This impedes an effective resource allocation to different workloads submitted to the database. We propose to obviate the need for possibly wrong optimizer decisions regarding physical join operators by replacing the traditional join algorithms by a single one which provides a performance at least as good as that of the most appropriate traditional join algorithm. *Generalized join* (g-join) combines the advantages of sort-merge join (exploits interesting orders), hash join (exploits different input sizes and fast probing for join partners), and index nested-loops join (exploits persistent indexes). The experimental comparison of g-join and the traditional join algorithms proves its competitiveness.

Third, we turn our attention toward modern architectures with increasing core numbers and main memory capacity. We develop a suite of *massively parallel sort-merge* (MPSM) joins that aim at exploiting the parallelization potential of multi-core processors in order to improve response times of analytical queries. We cover a disk-based highly parallel join algorithm for scenarios in which intermediate data must be written to disk, and a range-partitioned main memory join algorithm addressing the challenges of non-uniform memory access (NUMA) architectures. MPSM works on independently created runs in parallel, thereby avoiding synchronization. It scales almost linearly with the number of employed cores and is unsusceptible to data skew, which is indispensable for robust query processing. In a comparative experimental evaluation, MPSM clearly outperforms competing hash join proposals.

Contents

1	**Introduction**	**15**
	1.1 Problem Statement	16
	1.2 Contributions	17
	1.3 Outline	19
2	**Synergy-based Workload Management**	**21**
	2.1 Introduction	22
	2.2 Related Work	23
	2.3 Basic Approach	24
	2.3.1 Monitoring of Execution Times	24
	2.3.2 Architecture	24
	2.3.3 Training and Optimization Phases	25
	2.4 Synergy-based Scheduling	26
	2.4.1 Synergy Computation	27
	2.4.2 Example	28
	2.4.3 Scheduling in the Training Phase	29
	2.4.4 Scheduling in the Optimization Phase	31
	2.5 Simulation	32
	2.5.1 Simulation Framework	32
	2.5.2 Benchmark Settings	33
	2.5.3 Training Phase	35
	2.5.4 Optimization Phase	38
	2.6 Synergies in State-of-the-Art Database Systems	40
	2.7 Summary and Conclusions	43
3	**Robust Query Execution – The Generalized Join Algorithm**	**45**
	3.1 Introduction	46

- 3.2 Basic Algorithm 48
  - 3.2.1 Overview 49
  - 3.2.2 Data Structures and Page Processing 50
  - 3.2.3 Example 52
- 3.3 G-Join in Detail 54
  - 3.3.1 Detailed Algorithm 54
  - 3.3.2 Design Alternatives 58
  - 3.3.3 Outer, Semi, Anti Semi Joins 64
- 3.4 Traditional Join Algorithms 65
  - 3.4.1 Hash Join 65
  - 3.4.2 (Sort-)Merge Join 66
  - 3.4.3 Index Nested-Loops Join 67
  - 3.4.4 Summary and Comparison 68
- 3.5 Evaluation 70
  - 3.5.1 Settings 70
  - 3.5.2 G-Join vs. Traditional Join Algorithms 71
  - 3.5.3 Design Alternatives 76
  - 3.5.4 Memory Requirements 82
- 3.6 G-Join Relatives: G-Distinct and G-Aggregation 86
  - 3.6.1 Basic Algorithm 86
  - 3.6.2 Algorithm Details 87
  - 3.6.3 Example 90
  - 3.6.4 Traditional Grouping Algorithms 92
  - 3.6.5 Summary and Comparison 93
- 3.7 Summary and Conclusions 95

4 Massively Parallel Sort-Merge Joins 97
- 4.1 Introduction 98
- 4.2 A Family of MPSM Algorithms 101
  - 4.2.1 The Basic MPSM (B-MPSM) Algorithm 102
  - 4.2.2 The Memory Constrained Disk-enabled MPSM (D-MPSM) Algorithm 104
  - 4.2.3 The Range-Partitioned MPSM (P-MPSM) Algorithm 105
- 4.3 The MPSM Phases in Detail 106
  - 4.3.1 Partitioning the Private Input (Phase 2) 106
  - 4.3.2 Sorting the Private and Public Inputs (Phases 1 and 3) .. 109
  - 4.3.3 Join Phase (Phase 4) 110
- 4.4 Skew Resilience of P-MPSM 111
  - 4.4.1 Global S Data Distribution (Phase 2.1) 113
  - 4.4.2 Global R Data Distribution Histogram (Phase 2.2) 114
  - 4.4.3 Partitioning the Private Input R (Phase 2.3) 115
- 4.5 Beyond Inner MPSM and Two-Way Joins 116
  - 4.5.1 Outer, Semi, Anti Semi Joins 117
  - 4.5.2 The Guy Lohman Test 120
- 4.6 Experimental Evaluation 128
  - 4.6.1 Platform and Benchmark Scenarios 128
  - 4.6.2 Evaluation of MPSM for Inner Joins 129
  - 4.6.3 Performance Comparison of Inner, Outer, Semi, and Anti Semi MPSM Joins 134

  4.6.4 Exploiting MPSM Characteristics in Complex Query Plans 135
 4.7 Related Work 140
 4.8 Summary and Conclusions 141

5 Summary and Conclusions 143

Bibliography 147

List of Figures

1.1	Concurrent execution of OLAP and OLTP workloads in a database management system	16
2.1	Execution of analytical workloads in a database management system . . .	22
2.2	Architecture of the optimization component	25
2.3	Adaptive switching between training and optimization	26
2.4	Development of the shares and the synergy matrix	29
2.5	Example data for training algorithms	31
2.6	Simulation workload setting: query types and their (anti-)synergies	34
2.7	Synergy values for the simulation workload	35
2.8	Prediction error subject to the number of training queries and the training algorithm	36
2.9	Prediction error subject to the number of training queries and the training algorithm with a simulated execution time deviation of 30%	38
2.10	Effect of synergy exploitation and feedback during the optimization phase .	39
2.11	Execution time of different TPC-H-based workload schedules (runs) on DBMS-X (adapted from Wylezich (2011))	41
2.12	Synergy values for the TPC-H queries $Q1$, $Q2$, $Q9$, $Q3$, $Q4$, and $Q13$ on DBMS-X	42
3.1	Query processing in a relational database management system	46
3.2	Runs R_i and S_j with key ranges per page	50
3.3	G-join example: join phase	52
3.4	G-join example: join phase (cont'd)	53
3.5	Hybrid g-join	58
3.6	Overview of design alternatives for run generation, priority queues, build input, and probe input	59
3.7	Computation of "poor man's normalized key"	60

3.8	Illustration of the "last-run problem"	63
3.9	Hash join in HyPer/dbcore	65
3.10	Sort-merge join in HyPer/dbcore	67
3.11	Index nested-loops join in HyPer/dbcore	67
3.12	Sort-index nested-loops join in HyPer/dbcore	68
3.13	Extract of the TPC-C schema	71
3.14	Execution time comparison of g-join (GJ), hash join (HJ), and sort-merge join (MJ) on unsorted inputs	72
3.15	Execution time comparison of g-join (GJ), hash join (HJ), and sort-merge join (MJ) on roughly sorted inputs	73
3.16	Execution time comparison of g-join (GJ), hash join (HJ), and sort-merge join (MJ) when the optimizer wrongly assumes OrderLine to be the smaller relation	74
3.17	G-join and hash join execution times in-memory	75
3.18	Hybrid g-join (HGJ) smooths the execution time increase of g-join (GJ) when the data size slightly exceeds the memory size	76
3.19	Execution time comparison of g-join (GJ), index nested-loops join (NL), sort-index nested-loops join (SN), which sorts the probe input before joining, and hash join (HJ)	77
3.20	Execution time comparison of g-join using heap sort (HS), heap sort with poor man's normalized keys (HK), and replacement selection (RS) during run generation	78
3.21	Join phase execution time comparison of g-join using a hash table (HT), the ISAM* data structure (I*), a red-black tree (RB), and a splay tree (S) as in-memory index structure during the join phase	79
3.22	Execution time comparison of g-join on uniform data, on skewed Order data, and on skewed OrderLine data (scale 750)	80
3.23	Join phase execution time comparison of g-join using loser trees (LT), weak-heaps (WH), and heaps (H) as priority queues during the join phase	81
3.24	Average number of buffer pool frames per left input run during the join phase of g-join (scale 750)	82
3.25	G-join memory footprint (scale 750)	83
3.26	Average number of buffer pool frames per left input run during the join phase of g-join when omitting buffer pool growth limitation (scale 750)	85
3.27	Average number of buffer pool frames per left input run during the join phase of g-join when skipping processing of the first and last right input run and omitting buffer pool growth limitation (scale 750)	85
3.28	Representation of the hash table index structure	89
3.29	B-tree index structure	90
3.30	G-aggregation *count* example: run generation	90
3.31	G-aggregation *count* example: aggregation phase	91
3.32	G-aggregation *count* example: aggregation phase (cont'd)	92
4.1	Execution of an analytical query on a multi-core NUMA system	98
4.2	Impact of NUMA-affine versus NUMA-agnostic data processing	100
4.3	Comparison of basic join processing of Wisconsin hash join, radix join, and MPSM	101
4.4	B-MPSM join with four workers W_i	102

4.5	Disk-enabled MPSM join	104
4.6	P-MPSM join with four workers W_i	105
4.7	Phase 2 of P-MPSM	108
4.8	Radix sort	109
4.9	Integrated chunking and sorting	110
4.10	Interpolation search	110
4.11	Refined phase 2 of P-MPSM	112
4.12	P-MPSM CDF computation	113
4.13	Fine-grained histograms at little overhead	114
4.14	Outer and anti semi P-MPSM join with four workers W_i	117
4.15	Outer and anti semi join processing require attention during the join phase	118
4.16	Semi P-MPSM join with four workers W_i	119
4.17	Result of P-MPSM join with four workers W_i	121
4.18	Example of generalized MPSM teams for join and aggregation	124
4.19	Example of generalized MPSM teams for multi-way join and aggregation	127
4.20	HyPer1: Linux server with 1 TB main memory and four Intel CPUs with 8 physical cores (16 hardware contexts) each	128
4.21	Performance comparison of MPSM, Vectorwise (VW), and Wisconsin hash join on uniform data	130
4.22	Scalability of MPSM and Vectorwise	131
4.23	Effect of role reversal on join execution time	132
4.24	Effect of location skew on MPSM performance	133
4.25	Effect of balancing splitters on MPSM performance	134
4.26	Performance comparison of inner (I), left outer (LO), right outer (RO), left semi (LS), right semi (RS), left anti semi (LA), and right anti semi (RA) MPSM join	135
4.27	Performance comparison of two subsequent MPSM join executions and two independent MPSM joins	136
4.28	Two subsequent MPSM joins exploiting the rough sort order of the intermediate result runs	137
4.29	Performance comparison of two subsequent MPSM joins without postprocessing the intermediate result (2 MPSM), with merging each worker's intermediate result runs (Merge), and with concatenating the intermediate result runs (Concat)	139
4.30	Performance comparison of two subsequent MPSM joins without postprocessing the intermediate result (2 MPSM) and pipelined MPSM (16 workers)	139
5.1	Combining the approaches for efficient, robust, and scalable OLAP query processing	146

List of Tables

2.1	Simulated sources of synergies	32
2.2	Parameters for database simulation	33
2.3	Approaches to exploit sources of synergies (adapted from Wylezich (2011))	40
2.4	Correlation between synergy values and execution times of different TPC-H workload schedules	42
3.1	Classification of inputs to a query optimizer	47
3.2	Join algorithms and the input properties they exploit (adapted from Graefe (2012))	47
3.3	Characteristics of hash join, sort-merge join, and g-join in HyPer/dbcore	69
3.4	Data scales and sizes for the experiments	71
3.5	Analysis of run generation alternatives heap sort (HS), heap sort with poor man's normalized keys (HK), and replacement selection (RS) with respect to key comparisons (scale 750)	78
3.6	Analysis of priority queue alternatives loser trees (LT), heaps (H), and weak-heaps (WH) with respect to key comparisons (scale 750)	81
3.7	MB-seconds of g-join, hash join, and sort-merge join for unsorted inputs with different scales	83
3.8	Statistics about right input runs (scale 750)	84
3.9	Characteristics of traditional hash-based grouping, traditional sort-based grouping, and g-aggregation	94
4.1	Multiplicities and resulting data sizes for the experiments	129
4.2	Number of inner (I), pure left outer (LO), pure right outer (RO), left semi (LS), right semi (RS), left anti semi (LA), and right anti semi (RA) result tuples for the tested datasets	135

List of Algorithms

3.1	g-join for unsorted and unindexed inputs larger than memory	49
3.2	process-page of right input run during join phase	51
3.3	g-join complete algorithm	55
3.4	in-memory-join for $buildInput \leq$ available main memory	55
3.5	assign-roles assigns build and probe input roles to inputs	56
3.6	join phase of g-join	57
3.7	g-aggregation for unsorted input and output larger than memory	87
4.1	Splitter computation (adapted from Ross and Cieslewicz (2009))	116

Chapter 1

Introduction

Database management systems are typically confronted with a multitude of different workloads at a time. These workloads can be categorized into transactional workloads denoted as *Online Transaction Processing* (OLTP) and analytical workloads called *Online Analytical Processing* (OLAP). OLTP workloads realize the operational, i.e., day-to-day business, and typically consist of rather simple and short-running queries processing only a small part of the recent data. On the other hand, OLAP workloads form the basis of business intelligence applications and consist of complex, long-running queries processing large portions of (mostly historical) data. While OLTP workloads must be processed at a high throughput rate, for OLAP queries the focus is on response time. Because of the very different characteristics and requirements of these workloads, they were separated in the past: OLTP workloads were run against transactional database systems, while OLAP workloads were processed by data warehouse systems. This separation allowed for a dedicated optimized physical design of the systems and guaranteed that resource intensive OLAP queries would not affect the OLTP throughput. However, analytical results were obtained based on possibly outdated data. In today's fast-paced times, the freshness of information is crucial for strategic planning. The emerging demand for real-time business intelligence finally led to the reintegration of OLTP and OLAP workloads within one system. That is, transactional and analytical queries are run against the companies' up-to-date operational databases at the same time. Now, the challenge is to process complex and long-running OLAP workloads in a way that leaves enough resources for time-critical OLTP workloads. This work focuses on the efficient and robust processing of OLAP workloads to achieve this goal.

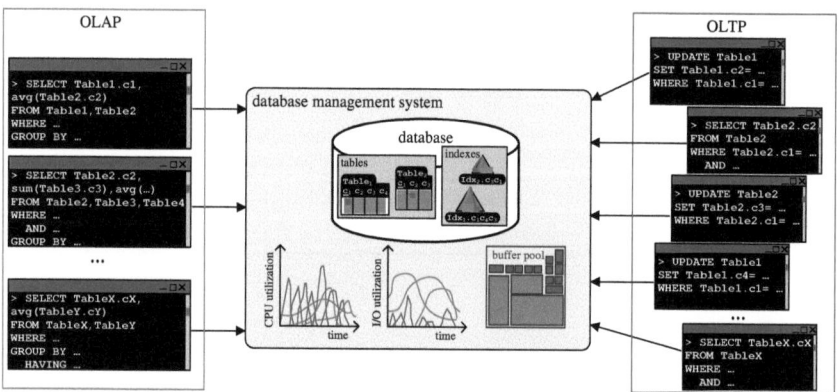

Figure 1.1: Concurrent execution of OLAP and OLTP workloads in a database management system: long-running and computation-intensive OLAP queries incur high CPU and I/O load and use large parts of the buffer pool – they are competing for the resources with the short-running and time-critical OLTP transactions

1.1 Problem Statement

Operational database systems are optimized for processing OLTP transactions at a high throughput. However, they now face the necessity to efficiently handle both analytical and transactional workloads at the same time. Heavy OLAP queries providing important information for business reports and continuously submitted OLTP transactions constituting the operational business differ greatly with respect to response time, data access behavior, and resource utilization. They compete for the system's CPUs, I/O bandwidth, and buffer pool frames. This scenario is illustrated in Figure 1.1.

The additional load on the database system introduced by the concurrent OLAP processing needs to be limited in order to affect OLTP performance as little as possible. In the first place, this requires a very (time) efficient execution of OLAP workloads. That way, the load on the database system is reduced and the free database resources can be used for OLTP processing. Furthermore, by minimizing the execution time of OLAP workloads, the obtained OLAP query results deliver useful information to business intelligence applications within short response times, which enables an effective strategic planning. As analytical queries are typically executed in batches, techniques of multi-query optimization are applicable. The goal of these techniques is to minimize the total execution time of the OLAP workload by exploiting characteristics of the workload queries to save work.

OLAP queries conduct complex computations on huge amounts of data and are thus long-running and resource-intensive. When there is a high variance in their execution times, the unpredictable load on the database system caused by the OLAP workloads prevents an effective allocation of resources to transactional and analytical workloads. Also, unstable response time performance of the system leads to users of business intelligence applications being unsatisfied. This is why, besides execution time, robust query execution with predictable performance is of great interest, too. Query performance in relational database systems heavily relies on the execution plan chosen by the database optimizer. Poor optimization of a complex OLAP query leads to unexpectedly bad execution behavior and causes additional resource contention within the database system. An approach to achieving robust query execution therefore is to avoid disadvantageous query optimizer decisions.

Optimized resource management and efficient query processing are significant in order to handle a high arrival rate of OLTP transactions and to answer OLAP queries quickly within a single database system. However, they can only be leveraged up to a certain level, and increasing requirements make it inevitable – at some point – to scale the underlying hardware with respect to main memory capacity and processing cores. The additional resources must be used by the database system in an effective way to serve the needs of both OLTP and OLAP clients and to achieve scalable performance. In particular, OLAP query processing can profit greatly from intra-query parallelism within database operators. However, simply porting existing algorithms to parallel environments and main memory databases, possibly with underlying non-uniform memory access (NUMA) architecture, may result in a totally unbalanced load and thus in suboptimal and, in particular, in unpredictable execution times. Shifting query processing within database systems from single-threaded and disk-based to highly parallel and in-memory processing requires database algorithms to be revised to make efficient use of modern hardware with multiple cores per socket and huge main memory.

To sum it up, OLAP workloads consist of very data-intensive and complex queries and cause heavy load in the database system. They are executed on transactional databases as up-to-date information is decisive for the strategic planning of companies. At the same time, guaranteeing the required OLTP throughput is crucial for the day-to-day business. The database system must allocate and use resources in a way such that OLAP workloads provide the requested data promptly and enough resources are still available for processing the OLTP workloads. A prerequisite to achieving this goal is to execute analytical workloads efficiently and to provide robust query performance while taking advantage of additional resources in query processing.

1.2 Contributions

This work examines three different approaches to the efficient, robust, and scalable execution of analytical workloads:

Synergy-based workload management focuses on the interplay of multiple queries within an OLAP workload. The concurrently executed queries may have a positive impact on the execution of each other, e.g., due to caching or complementary resource consumption, or they may impede each other's execution, e.g., in the case of resource contention. By exploiting positive impacts and avoiding negative ones, the execution time of OLAP workloads and thus the time they occupy resources can be minimized. Both positive and negative impacts are reflected by the execution time of the workload. For instance, positive caching impacts imply less I/O overhead and result in a shorter execution time. On the other hand, contention for main memory is a negative impact which leads to thrashing and increased I/O and thus to a longer execution time. The influence of a query on another query – we call this the *synergy* between the two queries – depends on a multitude of factors, e.g., the system's hardware and configuration, implementation details of the database operators, and programs running on the same system as the database. Thus, the prediction of query influences is a complex task and prediction models are often based on probably arguable assumptions. We present a different approach considering the database as a black box. By monitoring the execution times of different query sets at runtime, we draw conclusions regarding the synergies of queries. This information can also instantly be applied by the scheduling component in order to maximize efficiency of OLAP workload execution. In contrast to prior work, our approach does not focus on a certain source of synergy and does not require an offline phase for information gathering. Using a simulation framework, we evaluate our approach and find that it is capable of quickly detecting synergies and of exploiting those synergies. We further show that our approach is applicable to analytical workloads run on a commercial database system.

Robust query execution concentrates on the efficient and predictable behavior of single database queries. In order to effectively allocate resources to different workloads submitted to the database, it is necessary to ensure a certain predictability of query execution. For query execution to be predictable, each of the query's execution plan operators needs to perform in a calculable way. In this work, we examine the join operator, a central operator to OLAP-style queries. Due to outdated statistics or mistaken optimizer decisions, join execution might be far from optimal and, in particular, not predictable at all in terms of both duration and resource utilization. We propose to obviate the need for possibly wrong optimizer decisions regarding physical join operators by replacing the traditional join algorithms by a single one which provides a performance at least as good as the most appropriate traditional join algorithm. *Generalized join* (g-join) combines the advantages of sort-merge join (exploits interesting orders), hash join (exploits different input sizes and fast probing for join partners), and index nested-loops join (exploits persistent indexes). We present the g-join algorithm and discuss and evaluate different design decisions and their performance impacts. Further, we conduct an experimental comparison of g-join and the traditional join algorithms proving its competitiveness.

Massively parallel sort-merge join algorithms provide scalable analytical query execution tailored to modern hardware architectures with increasing core numbers and main memory capacity. The developments in hardware lead to a shift in database processing from single-threaded and I/O-bound to multi-threaded and in-memory. The additional resources can, in particular, be employed to speed up analytical query processing. In order to make effective use of parallel processing and in-memory data, the traditional query processing needs to be revised. In particular, the non-uniform memory access (NUMA) behavior of modern main memory architectures needs to be considered. We develop a suite of *massively parallel sort-merge* (MPSM) joins, which is carefully designed to meet the challenges of modern hardware. MPSM works on independently created runs in parallel and avoids synchronization. Thereby, it exploits the parallelization potential of multi-core processors best in order to improve response times of analytical queries. We devise a disk-based MPSM variant for scenarios in which intermediate data must be written to disk, and a range-partitioned main memory MPSM variant. The presented algorithms are unsusceptible to data skew, which is indispensable for robust query processing. MPSM scales almost linearly with the number of cores and thus allows an effective use of additional processing resources with predictable effects. We conduct a comparative experimental evaluation and show that MPSM clearly outperforms competing hash join proposals. Further, we investigate MPSM for non-inner joins and in multi-join scenarios for a comprehensive study.

1.3 Outline

This thesis is organized as follows:

- Chapter 2 covers our approach for synergy-based workload management. We define synergies between queries and describe how they can be derived from measured execution times. Then, we show how synergies can be exploited for the synergy-based scheduling of OLAP workloads. We evaluate the approach using a simulation framework and show how it can be applied to real database scenarios.

- Chapter 3 presents and evaluates the g-join operator as a robust alternative to traditional join operators. We depict design alternatives and discuss their impact on robustness and performance. Further, we prove the competitiveness of g-join compared to traditional join algorithms in an extensive experimental evaluation.

- Chapter 4 investigates the challenges that NUMA architectures pose to the design of database algorithms. Based on our findings, we then introduce a suite of massively parallel sort-merge (MPSM) join algorithms for main memory multi-core database systems and evaluate them. We show that, by careful design, MPSM achieves linear scalability in the number of cores and outperforms current state-of-the art parallel join algorithms by factors.

- Chapter 5 concludes the thesis and gives an outlook how the presented techniques can be combined to achieve the goal of efficient, robust, and scalable execution of analytical workloads.

Chapter 2

Synergy-based Workload Management

Analytical workloads consist of complex and long-running queries which process large portions of the database. In order to affect the performance of transactional workloads being processed concurrently within the same database system as little as possible, the execution of these analytical workloads needs to be efficient with respect to time and resources. Most database systems execute multiple queries of one workload in parallel in order to best utilize the available system resources like processors and main memory. The concurrently executed queries may influence each other's execution either positively or negatively. By grouping together queries with positive effects and avoiding groups with negative effects, the overall performance of the database system can be improved. A vast number of approaches have been developed within this context, most of them belonging to one of two categories: analysis or monitoring. However, they mainly either focus only on one possible kind of impact of queries on each other's execution time (e.g., caching), or require an offline phase for information gathering.

In this chapter, we present a monitoring-based approach which does not require an offline phase and is not limited to a certain source of query impacts. It flexibly adapts to any database system or hardware configuration. Our approach bases on the fact that both positive and negative impacts of queries on each other's execution are reflected by the execution time of the workload. The impacts between request types are derived in a fully automated and database-transparent manner at runtime from the measured execution times of different query sets. The gained knowledge about impacts can further instantly be applied by the scheduling component in order to maximize the efficiency of the workload execution. Our approach works completely independently from changing synergies or configurations and easily handles new query types.

Parts of the work presented in this chapter appeared in Albutiu and Kemper (2009) and in Albutiu et al. (2009).

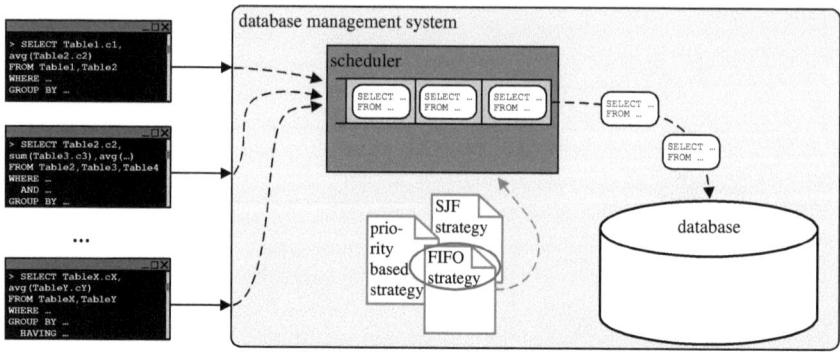

Figure 2.1: Execution of analytical workloads in a database management system: multiple queries are submitted to the database system concurrently where they are queued until the scheduler chooses them for execution based on a scheduling strategy as soon as system resources are available

2.1 Introduction

In database systems, queries are executed concurrently in order to provide a good utilization of the system's resources like processors and main memory. The number of parallel queries is typically limited to prevent the database from overload. As illustrated in Figure 2.1, requests submitted to the database system are not directly processed but intercepted and queued. As soon as system resources are available (i.e., freed by previously executed requests), the scheduler selects one or more queries from the queue to be executed next. It bases its decision on a scheduling strategy. A very simple strategy is to start queries in a first-in-first-out (FIFO) manner, i.e., the oldest query in the queue is admitted to the database first. This strategy is fair as queries are started in the order they arrive at the database system. However, more complex strategies can be employed in order to improve overall system performance.

We present a scheduling strategy which focuses on the interplay of multiple concurrently executed queries within a workload. The concurrently running queries may interact with each other and thus influence each other's execution time positively or negatively. A common example for positive interactions between queries running in a database system are caching effects. Negative interactions may occur in the case of resource contention. By detecting and exploiting positive influences between queries, the workload performance in the database system can be maximized. On the other hand, negative query combinations with high or unpredictable execution times can be avoided. The influence of a query on another query – we call this the *synergy* between the two queries – depends on a multitude of factors, like the system's hardware and configuration (e.g., available main memory and number of cores), implementation details of the database operators (e.g., in-place or not), and programs running on the same system as the database (and sharing the limited resources). They can be classified into resource-based, data-based, and query-based. Resource-based synergies refer to the efficient utilization of system resources like CPUs and buffer pools. Scheduling should be targeted at using the resources to full capacity but not overloading them. Data-based synergies appear when multiple queries process the same data and thus can profit from shared scanning or caching. Executing those queries at the same time or with little time-lag is beneficial. Query-based synergies occur when queries share parts of their execution plans. Such common subqueries can be optimized and executed only once, and intermediate results can be shared.

Most sources of synergies cannot clearly be assigned to one of these categories but have impacts on at least two of them. For instance, when common subexpressions (query-based synergy) can be exploited, no repeated optimization and execution of subqueries is conducted and this reduces both: the CPU utilization (resource-based synergy), as computations are only conducted once, and the number of disk accesses (data-based synergy), as the data is also read only once. Furthermore, the effects of different sources of synergies overlap and may cancel each other out. Thus, the prediction of query influences is a complex task and prediction models are often based on probably arguable assumptions.

We present a different approach considering the database system as a black box. We rely on the fact that both positive and negative synergies between queries are reflected by the execution time of these queries. By monitoring the execution times of different query sets at runtime, we draw conclusions regarding the synergies of the queries. This information can also instantly be applied by the scheduling component in order to maximize the efficiency of OLAP workload execution.

2.2 Related Work

Workload management, which includes scheduling techniques, is a part of many products like the HP Workload Manager for Neoview by HP (2007), the IBM Query Patroller for DB2 described by Niu et al. (2006), the Microsoft SQL Server by Microsoft (2007), and the Oracle Database Resource Manager by Oracle (2001). Krompass et al. (2008) present an overview of current workload management techniques and implementations. Common approaches for scheduling are FIFO and priority-based. However, none of the commercial products considers influences of queries on each other.

Approaches that take into account impacts of queries can be classified according to the technique of impact detection: those based on *analysis* examine the workload queries in order to determine sources of synergies. For example, common subqueries investigated by Choenni et al. (1997) and Subramanian and Venkataraman (1998) need only be optimized once for all the queries in which they occur. But also shared data is a source of performance gains, e.g., by using cooperative scans as introduced by Zukowski et al. (2007). Analysis techniques focus on one specific source of synergy, which is then exploited. However, there are a great number of different sources of positive and negative synergy to be taken into consideration, and they may also neutralize each other. Furthermore, the analysis of queries is often a complex task requiring a lot of information, which is not always provided by a database system. By contrast, approaches based on *monitoring* consider the database system and the queries as black boxes. Information is gained by observing the execution of queries and drawing conclusions. O'Gorman et al. (2002) compare the number of disk accesses for the pairwise sequential and concurrent execution of queries defined by the TPC-H benchmark. That way, they identify caching effects without analyzing the underlying data of both queries. However, this approach only detects pairwise synergies and requires the synergy detection to take place before the actual scheduling.

An approach which is similar to ours in terms of the computational model is that of Ahmad et al. (2008). However, their approach is only applicable to batch workloads and it requires an offline sampling phase. As opposed to that, our approach focuses on the optimization of continuous workloads and acquires knowledge during the online phase.

2.3 Basic Approach

Our approach for the detection and exploitation of query synergies is totally independent from the database system used, takes into consideration all sources of synergies, and is transparent to the clients issuing the database requests. In this section, we present the underlying principles of the approach and the architecture of the optimization component.

2.3.1 Monitoring of Execution Times

We focus on a monitoring approach which considers the database system as well as the executed queries as black boxes. That is, we do not analyze the structure of requests and cannot anticipate their resource requirements. Furthermore, no information about the configuration of the database system or its current load is available. Only measurements that can be obtained by monitoring the system serve as input to the optimization model. We choose to use execution time as an indicator for the overall synergy of queries rather than, e.g., CPU load or number of cache misses. Measuring one of those bears the risk of strictly focusing on one certain source of synergy and missing other influential factors. For instance, a low CPU utilization does not provide any information about the buffer pool utilization. Both thrashing (continuously triggering page loading as a result of buffer pool over-utilization) and execution of I/O-bound queries (under-utilizing the buffer pool while waiting for slow disk operations) result in the same low CPU load measurement and thus cannot be distinguished. By contrast, the execution time of queries is affected by all influences in combination. A short overall execution time indicates that the order in which the workload queries are executed permits to exploit sources of synergies like caching and, at the same time, avoids counterproductive effects like resource contention. Although it is not obvious what the sources of synergies are, the main goal of scheduling, i.e., minimizing the workload execution time, is met. Our approach therefore considers execution time as the main indicator for good, i.e., synergy-aware, scheduling.

2.3.2 Architecture

In order to realize the approach in a database independent way, we use the architecture depicted in Figure 2.2: A middleware layer between client and database intercepts the client requests and forwards them to the optimization component. This middleware layer can be realized as a wrapper around the database driver, e.g., a modified JDBC driver for Java clients which falls back on a database-specific JDBC driver for establishing database connections and sending requests to the database. The optimization component first classifies the requests, i.e., determines the type of each request. The classification identifies queries only differing in parameter values but having the same SQL skeleton. Those queries are assigned the same type. Under certain assumptions like uniformly distributed data, queries having the same type will have the same execution characteristics (like CPU-intensive, short-running, etc.). However, in case of skewed data, this assumption

2.3 Basic Approach

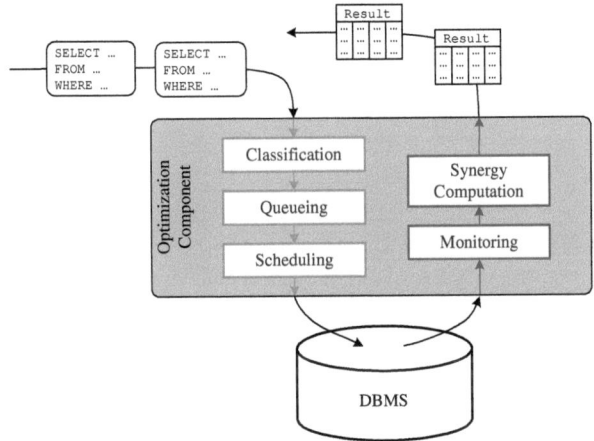

Figure 2.2: Architecture of the optimization component

may not apply as Reddy and Haritsa (2005) demonstrate. A query q being short-running with parameter $x \in [0, 100]$ may become long-running with parameter $y \in [101, 110]$. The approach can easily handle such a case by including parameter values into the classification process, thus forming two types of queries q_1 and q_2 out of the SQL skeleton of q for the intervals $[0, 100]$ and $[101, 110]$, respectively. x and y can be determined using 2D classification techniques. The classified queries are then queued in the middleware. Whenever the database can accept new requests, a scheduling algorithm determines a set of queries out of the queue to be executed next. The size of the set is determined in advance such that the database load is maximized. After the execution of the query set has finished, the monitored execution time is fed back into the optimization component where the synergies are computed. The interception of queries by the optimization component is completely transparent to both clients and database system.

2.3.3 Training and Optimization Phases

The approach consists of two phases: the *training phase* and the *optimization phase*. Depending on the phase, different scheduling algorithms are applied. During training, the main goal of scheduling is to determine synergies between queries. By executing certain combinations of queries, we intend to obtain a broad knowledge about the queries' influences on each other within short time. Here, the optimization of database performance is of secondary importance. In order to avoid the risk of missing yet unknown even higher synergies, we don't make use of already known synergies in the scheduling of the training phase. As the scheduling algorithms aim at maximal knowledge acquisition about all query types, the workload performance during the training phase is not affected negatively compared to random or FIFO scheduling. Having learned about the synergies between queries of the workload, scheduling during the optimization phase makes use of them in order to minimize the total execution time. That is, those queries yielding the highest positive synergies are executed together. In both phases, the knowledge base con-

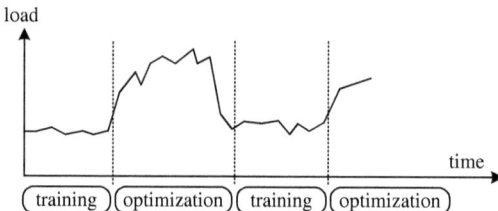

Figure 2.3: Adaptive switching between training and optimization depending on system load

sisting of different query combinations and their execution times is continuously extended by feeding back new monitoring data. If it is possible without performance decrease, new query combinations can also be tested during the optimization phase. That way, the possibly insufficient information can be completed even after the training phase has finished. Further, long-term changes in synergies can be detected and new query types can be integrated into the optimization.

There is no general best point in time for switching from training to optimization phase. It depends on the database workload and the system load as well as on the amount of synergy information already obtained. There exists a trade-off between completeness and accuracy of synergy information, and the duration of unoptimized scheduling. However, as new information is continuously fed into the model not only during training but also during optimization, yet incomplete synergy information may be completed later on. After finishing the training phase, the system is not limited to the knowledge gathered by that time, but keeps on collecting information and thereby even adapts to changing conditions. Furthermore, if load on the database system varies, it is possible to dynamically switch between training and optimization as illustrated in Figure 2.3. During low system load phases, the free resources are exploited for determining unknown or enhancing inaccurate synergy values. When system load is high, scheduling based on the detected synergies improves system performance.

2.4 Synergy-based Scheduling

We now describe how to derive synergy values from measured execution times. Then, we present our scheduling algorithms for the training and optimization phases. In this context, we assume the following scenario: Workloads consist of multiple instances of certain query types differing in parameter values. The queries are not dependent on the results of each other and thus can be reordered arbitrarily. In order to prevent the database from overload, the number of concurrently executed requests – called multi-programming level (MPL) – is limited. Determining a good MPL is crucial for database performance. We assume that a reasonable target MPL has been identified, e.g., using the methods described by Schroeder et al. (2006), and determine a good scheduling within the constraints of that given MPL.

2.4.1 Synergy Computation

In order to accurately determine influences of certain queries on others, we execute the queries of a workload blockwise, i.e., only after all queries of one block have finished execution, the next block is submitted to the database.

Within a block of MPL many queries, each of the queries influences the execution of each of the other block queries, either positively or negatively. In other words, there exist pairwise synergies between the queries of one concurrently executed block, which either result in a shorter overall execution time (if the synergies are mainly positive) or in a longer one (if they are mainly negative). Thus, the overall execution time of a block of queries (rt, response time) can be represented by a linear combination of $\binom{MPL}{2}$ execution time shares s_{xy} of two query types x and y. The execution time for a block of four concurrently executed queries of types a, b, c, and d is thus:

$$rt_{abcd} = s_{ab} + s_{ac} + s_{ad} + s_{bc} + s_{bd} + s_{cd}$$

Each share s_{xy} represents the influence that the concurrent execution of the queries x and y has on the overall execution time. The execution time shares are symmetric, i.e., $s_{xy} = s_{yx}$. If all of the block's queries have equal execution times and there are no synergies, the influences (shares) are equal. A block consisting of queries of different complexity (and thus different execution times) results in greater values of the shares containing complex queries and smaller values of the shares representing less complex queries. Further, if two of the queries have (positive) synergies, their share is smaller, which also results in a smaller response time of the block.

The synergy of a query x with respect to another query y is determined by putting their execution time share s_{xy} in relation to the execution time shares of x with all known query types. The set of known query types is denoted by Q and may increase during runtime. We define the synergy syn_{xy} between two queries x and y, i.e., the impact on the execution time of x caused by the concurrent execution of y, as the difference between the average execution time share of x with all other known query types q and the share of x and y:

$$syn_{xy} = \frac{\sum_{q \in Q} s_{xq}}{|Q|} - s_{xy}.$$

Yet unknown share values s_{xy} distort the computed synergy as subtracting 0 from $\frac{\sum_{q \in Q} s_{xq}}{|Q|}$ will result in the highest possible synergy value syn_{xy}. This is why we assume unknown values s_{xy} to be equal to the average of all known values $s_{xk}, k \in Q$, containing query type x, so that the resulting synergy is 0. Contrary to the execution time shares, the synergy between two query types is not symmetric, i.e., $syn_{xy} \neq syn_{yx}$ in general. Query x may benefit more from the concurrent execution of query y than the other way round, e.g., if the data needed by y is a superset of the data needed by x and caching is the main source of synergy. The determined synergy values syn_{xy} are represented as a matrix with rows x and columns y, called the *synergy matrix*.

In order to determine accurate values of the execution time shares, each query pair is executed in several combinations with other query types in Q, thus collecting a number of response time values that form a linear system of equations of the following form:

$$rt_{abcd} = s_{ab} + s_{ac} + s_{ad} + s_{bc} + s_{bd} + s_{cd} + e_{abcd}$$

The slack variable e_{abcd} accounts for measurement errors or execution time fluctuations. If a combination is executed repeatedly, the response time value rt is set to the average of the measured execution times. Thereby, the model adapts to execution time variations, which may be accidentally (e.g., due to external influences) or reasonable (e.g., if the system configuration has been changed). The execution of new combinations provides new equations to the system, thereby allowing a more precise solution to be determined.

By definition, solving a linear system of equations with n unknowns requires n equations. In our case, if we assume that $|Q| = 5$ there are $\binom{5}{2}+5 = 15$ different shares (of which $\binom{5}{2}$ are of the form s_{xy} with $x \neq y$ and 5 are of the form s_{xx}). Without considering the slack variables, this would require 15 different combinations to be executed. From our example above one can conclude that at the beginning of the workload execution, nearly every combination will contribute a few new unknowns and just one equation. Therefore, the linear system of equations is generally under-determined and requires an optimization objective. We employ the principle of maximum entropy proposed by Markl et al. (2007) for estimating selectivities of composed predicates. Following this principle, we include all of the collected knowledge about combination execution times in the computation but don't make any further assumptions. The uncertainty due to the under-determination of the system of equations is distributed equally over the variables. Our objective function thus has two goals: to equally distribute the execution time over the different execution time shares and to minimize the slack variables:

$$opt = min \left\{ \frac{\sigma(S)}{avg(S)} + \sum_{e \in E} e \right\},$$

where σ denotes the standard deviation, S is the set of all shares s_{xy}, E is the set of all slack variables e, and $avg(S) = \frac{1}{|S|} \sum_{s_{xy} \in S} s_{xy}$.

The coefficient of variation $\frac{\sigma(S)}{avg(S)}$ models the equal distribution of the execution time over the shares. The error sum $\sum_{e \in E} e$ ensures that the slack variables are minimized.

2.4.2 Example

The following example briefly demonstrates the approach. We assume that the MPL is set to three and the system knows of four different query types a, b, c, and d by now. First, the combination consisting of the types a, b, and c is executed in 200 time units. This results in the first equation:

$$rt_{abc} = s_{ab} + s_{ac} + s_{bc} + e_{abc} = 200$$

The solution of this system of equations is $s_{ab} = s_{ac} = s_{bc} = 67$ as shown in Figure 2.4a. As enforced by the objective function, the uncertainty is equally distributed over the variables contributing to the equation. All other variables are still unknown. The next block consists of the query types a, b, and d and is finished in 180 time units. The corresponding equation is:

$$rt_{abd} = s_{ab} + s_{ad} + s_{bd} + e_{abd} = 180$$

The solution of the new system of equations is shown in Figure 2.4b: $s_{ab} = 63$, $s_{ac} = 68$, $s_{bc} = 68$, $s_{ad} = 58$, and $s_{bd} = 58$.

2.4 Synergy-based Scheduling

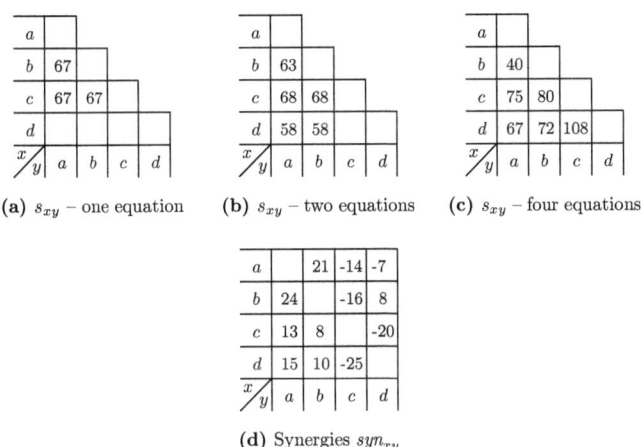

Figure 2.4: Development of the shares and the synergy matrix

At this point, it can already be noticed that the shares s_{ad}, s_{bd}, and s_{ab} contribute to the response time of the combinations with smaller values than the shares s_{ac} and s_{bc}. This indicates that the corresponding query pairs have greater synergies. After executing another two combinations containing a, c, and d, respectively b, c, and d, the system of equations is extended as follows:

$$rt_{acd} = s_{ac} + s_{ad} + s_{cd} + e_{acd} = 250$$

$$rt_{bcd} = s_{bc} + s_{bd} + s_{cd} + e_{bcd} = 260$$

Furthermore, the combination a, b, and c is executed a second time, with a measured time of 190 time units. The equation system is updated by computing the average value of rt for the first equation:

$$rt_{abc} = s_{ab} + s_{ac} + s_{bc} + e_{abc} = 195$$

The resulting shares are given in Figure 2.4c and the synergies computed out of these shares are shown in Figure 2.4d. There is a high positive synergy between the types a and b, which is also indicated by the small values of the shares containing a and b: $syn_{ab} = 21$ and $syn_{ba} = 24$. As stated above, the influence of a query type x on another type y is not necessarily equal to the influence of y on x. In the example computation, c benefits from the concurrent execution of a ($syn_{ca} = 13$) while a is penalized by the parallel processing of c ($syn_{ac} = -14$).

2.4.3 Scheduling in the Training Phase

The scheduling algorithms during both the training and the optimization phase determine a group of MPL many queries to be executed next. During training, the main scheduling goal is to gather as much information as possible about synergies, i.e., to best fill the synergy matrix. This is done by systematically executing different query combinations and monitoring their execution times. Each of the monitored combination execution times provides either a new equation (and thus at least one new value in the synergy matrix) or contributes to a more meaningful average execution time of an already executed combination (and thus results in more precise values in the synergy matrix). We examined the following different scheduling algorithms for training:

FIFO The queries are executed in the order in which they arrive.

MinUnknown The goal of this strategy is to fill the synergy matrix with as precise values as possible by selecting combinations of queries for which most of the variables in the system of equations are known.

MaxUnknown The goal of this strategy is to quickly fill the synergy matrix by selecting combinations of queries which provide the most new synergy values. In contrast to the *MinUnknown* strategy, the detected values may be quite imprecise because they rely on a small set of combinations.

MinComb This strategy selects combinations which have been executed the rarest. Following this strategy, the matrix will be enhanced by at least one new value after each combination execution. After each of the combinations has been executed at least once, the combinations' execution times are updated uniformly.

MinCombMinUnknown The goal of this strategy is to combine the goals of *MinComb* and *MinUnknown*, i.e., to fill the matrix with precise values and uniformly update the system of equations. It therefore favors combinations which have not yet been executed (often) and consist of a minimum number of unknown shares. This guarantees that the same combinations are not executed again and again as this does not add new equations to the system and therefore no additional information for the computation of new synergies.

MinCombMaxUnknown The goal of this strategy is to combine the goals of *MinComb* and *MaxUnknown*, i.e., to quickly fill the matrix and uniformly update the system of equations. Analogous to *MinCombMinUnknown*, this strategy favors rare combinations, however with many unknown shares.

In the example in Figure 2.5, two combinations abc and abd have already been executed. Therefore, the shares s_{ab}, s_{ac}, s_{bc}, s_{ad}, and s_{bd} are known. The queue contains the query types a, b, c, d, and e, so that the query combinations listed in Figure 2.5c may be executed next. The different scheduling algorithms result in the following choices:

Scheduling algorithm	Choice	Explanation
FIFO	abc	order in the queue
MinUnknown	abc	minimal number (0) of unknown shares
MaxUnknown	cde	maximal number (3) of unknown shares: s_{cd}, s_{ce}, s_{de}
MinComb	abe	minimal number (0) of executions
MinCombMinUnknown	acd	minimal number (0) of executions and unknown shares
MinCombMaxUnknown	cde	minimal number (0) of executions and maximal number (3) of unknown shares: s_{cd}, s_{ce}, s_{de}

2.4 Synergy-based Scheduling

combination	shares
abc	s_{ab}, s_{ac}, s_{bc}
abd	s_{ab}, s_{ad}, s_{bd}

(a) Already executed combinations and known shares

e	d	c	b	a

(b) Queued query types

combination	known shares	unknown shares	# executions
abc	s_{ab}, s_{ac}, s_{bc}		1
abd	s_{ab}, s_{ad}, s_{bd}		1
abe	s_{ab}	s_{ae}, s_{be}	0
acd	s_{ac}, s_{ad}	s_{cd}	0
ace	s_{ac}	s_{ae}, s_{ce}	0
ade	s_{ad}	s_{ae}, s_{de}	0
bcd	s_{bc}, s_{bd}	s_{cd}	0
bce	s_{bc}	s_{be}, s_{ce}	0
bde	s_{bd}	s_{be}, s_{de}	0
cde		s_{cd}, s_{ce}, s_{de}	0

(c) Enumeration of possible combinations, their known and unknown shares, and the number of times they have been executed

Figure 2.5: Example data for training algorithms (MPL=3)

2.4.4 Scheduling in the Optimization Phase

During the optimization phase, the workload is executed as efficiently as possible based on the knowledge gathered during the training. The main scheduling goal is to exploit the queries' synergies by selecting the query combinations to be executed based on the synergy matrix. In addition, monitoring data is still collected so that insufficient information is completed and long-term changes are detected. During the optimization, the following strategy is used:

The scheduling algorithm *MaxSyn* chooses the combination c of queries with the highest combination synergy syn_c, which is computed as follows using the synergies of the contained query pairs:

$$syn_c = \sum_{s_{xy} \in c} \left(syn_{xy} + syn_{yx} \right)$$

Some of the queries may have positive synergies, while others may influence each other's execution in a negative way. Positive and negative synergies between query pairs within a combination can cancel each other out. However, the combination containing the most synergetic query pairs has the highest combination synergy value. The computation of a complete schedule for the workload has exponential complexity and is thus not efficiently applicable. The *MaxSyn* strategy therefore employs a greedy approach which determines only one query combination to be executed at a time.[1]

---

[1] Please note that, in general, greedy approaches might lead to the problem of starvation. In the scenarios considered in this work, starvation cannot occur and is thus not addressed.

Source of synergy	Type	Simulation
Caching	positive	$caching(q_1, q_2) = c$, $c \in \mathcal{N}$, where c is the number of disk operations that can be saved due to caching advantages
Complementary resource requirements	positive	query types with complementary requirements of different resources
Resource contention	negative	query types with high requirements of the same resource
Lock contention	negative	decrease of processor share (and thus progress) by $locking(q_1, q_2) = l$, $l \in \mathcal{N}$
Memory thrashing	negative	limited database main memory, main memory requirements of query types, thrashing penalty

Table 2.1: Simulated sources of synergies

2.5 Simulation

We developed a database simulation framework which enables us (1) to evaluate different scheduling algorithms in a timely manner and (2) to verify the synergy matrix values. The second point is of particular importance as the presented approach is based on unsupervised learning and thus the solution cannot be validated using real data.

2.5.1 Simulation Framework

The simulation framework allows for modeling different types of queries, e.g., short-running, long-running, data-intensive, or processor-intensive. Further, a database system model is described by its cache size and resource capacities. Based on these parameters, the framework computes the execution time of the simulated queries corresponding to their resource requirements and impacts on each other. There are numerous sources of synergies. Some of them like caching are obvious while others are not. In our simulation framework, we had to choose a set of synergy sources on which to focus. Of course, this set is not complete but nevertheless, it provides a reasonable database simulation for our purposes. The following sources of (anti-)synergies are supported by the framework as described in Table 2.1: caching, complementary resource requirements, resource contention, lock contention, and memory thrashing.

Caching and complementary resource requirements are sources of positive synergy. Caching bypasses the slow disk access times and thus results in better performance. Further, if computation-intensive queries are executed concurrently with data-intensive queries, they don't affect each other negatively with respect to resources. On the contrary, their parallel execution results in a good utilization of the system resources. Resource and lock contention as well as memory thrashing are sources of negative synergy (anti-synergy). They prevent queries from progressing by not providing enough resource capacity and holding back needed data or paging it out of memory, respectively.

In the simulation framework, query types are identified by their total amount of used *processor cycles* and *disk operations*, and their required *main memory*. By varying the query type parameters, we can model computation-intensive queries like highly complex data analysis as well as disk-intensive queries reading a lot of data. A high main memory

2.5 Simulation

Parameter	Value
processor cycles per second	100
disk cycles per second	100
maximum processor quota per query	100
maximum disk quota per query	100
buffer pool size	21
out-of-RAM penalty	1

Table 2.2: Parameters for database simulation

value represents, e.g., query types containing sorting or other main-memory-intensive functions. Furthermore, we model the *cache synergies* and *lock anti-synergies* between queries as partial binary functions. The cache synergies of two query types q_1 and q_2 are given by $caching(q_1, q_2) = c$, $c \in \mathcal{N}$, where c is the number of disk operations that can be saved due to caching advantages. Lock anti-synergies are realized by reducing the number of processor cycles that can be assigned to a certain query by $locking(q_1, q_2) = l$, $l \in \mathcal{N}$. The simulated database is characterized by the processor and disk capacities, i.e., the *processor cycles* and *disk cycles* the database can perform per second, and the *buffer pool size*. Additional parameters are an *out-of-RAM penalty* and *maximum processor* and *disk quotas per query*. They allow for modeling memory thrashing and resource contention when combined with the query type parameters processor cycles, disk operations, and main memory requirements.

The execution of a set of queries is simulated by (1) computing each query's share of the system resources and (2) determining the queries' progress assuming they are assigned the computed shares. The first step is conducted for the current point in time based on the queries' requirements and impacts on other queries, and on the system parameters. In the second step, a short period of execution time is simulated during which the queries consume their resource shares. After that, the two steps are repeated for the new point in time.

2.5.2 Benchmark Settings

For our benchmarks, we used the database configuration given in Table 2.2 and defined a workload consisting of the five different query types described in Figures 2.6a to 2.6e. They have similar numbers of disk operations ranging from 50 to 72 units and require 3 to 8 units of main memory. Query type 5 has constant disk and processor requirements while the remaining query types have changing requirements during their execution. In Figures 2.6a to 2.6e, the ratio of processor and disk requirements over time is shown. Query types 1 and 2 are partly complementary with respect to processor and disk usage. Query types 3 and 4 exhibit similar processor and disk utilization, however, their main memory requirements differ greatly. The query types have more or less cache synergies and some of them have lock anti-synergies as shown in Figures 2.6f and 2.6g. We chose this workload to demonstrate the influences of resource requirements of different query types on how well they behave in combination.

Figure 2.7 shows the synergies for our benchmark workload. Query type 1 has the largest synergy value 592 with itself. This is because the required disk cycles and main

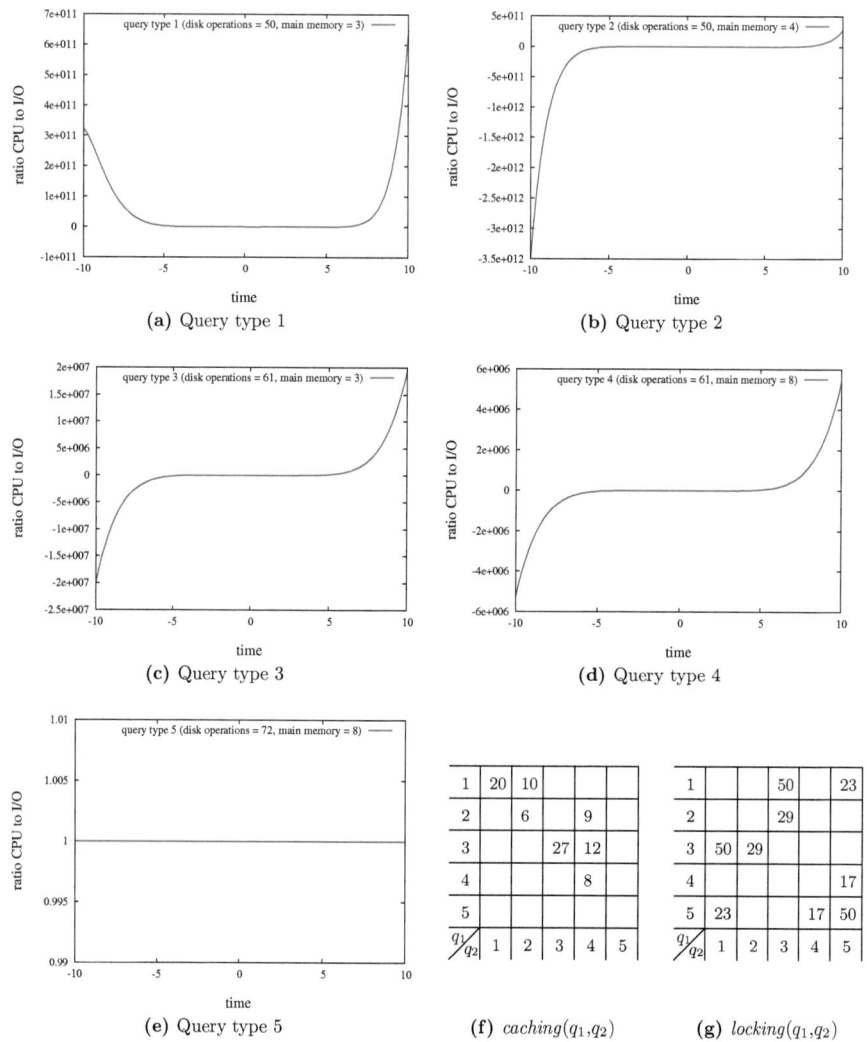

Figure 2.6: Simulation workload setting: query types and their (anti-)synergies

2.5 Simulation

$q_1 \backslash q_2$	1	2	3	4	5
1	592	193	-303	321	-803
2	102	-75	-428	374	27
3	-416	-450	360	465	37
4	106	250	363	-229	-494
5	-608	313	345	-84	32

Figure 2.7: Synergy values for the simulation workload

memory are moderate compared to the other query types. The smallest synergy value -803 of query types 1 and 5 can be explained by the high locking anti-synergies between the types. The same holds for query types 1 and 3. However, they compete less for main memory. Although types 3 and 4 are very similar in their processor cycle requirements compared to disk cycles, combining query type 3 with itself has much higher synergy values than combining query type 4 with itself. This is because of the higher main memory requirements of query type 4, which lead to thrashing.

We scale the workload size by uniformly adding queries of the different types. The workload is shuffled before each benchmark. Throughout the benchmarks, we employed an MPL of three.

2.5.3 Training Phase

We conducted a set of benchmarks in order to evaluate different training algorithms with respect to their ability to fill the synergy matrix quickly and with accurate values. The more accurate the values in the synergy matrix are, the more precisely we can predict the execution time of a certain combination of queries during the optimization phase, thereby enabling us to schedule the queued queries in a way that minimizes the total execution time. The quality measure we employ in order to evaluate the accuracy of the synergy matrix values is the deviation of the estimated execution time of a combination c, denoted by $\textit{est-rt}_c$, from the simulated (and later real) execution time $\textit{real-rt}_c$, which we call the *error coefficient* ec_c:

$$ec_c = \frac{|\textit{est-rt}_c - \textit{real-rt}_c|}{\textit{real-rt}_c}$$

The *prediction error* err_{pred} is defined as the average error coefficient ec_c over all possible query combinations of size MPL, denoted by the set C:

$$err_{pred} = \frac{1}{|C|} \sum_{c \in C} ec_c$$

As this measure is meaningful only after the matrix has been filled for the most part, we also consider a second measure, the *net prediction error*, which is computed the same way as the prediction error but only for non-empty matrix entries.

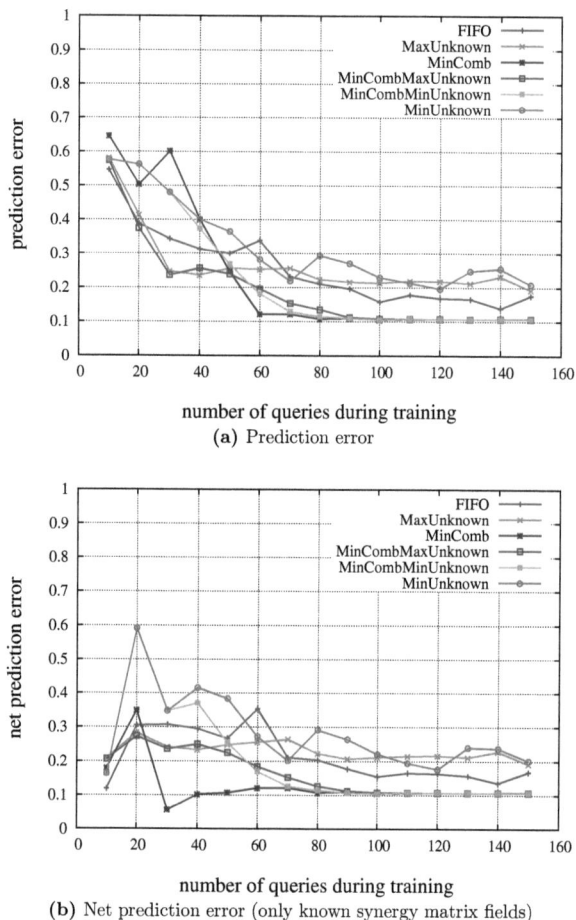

Figure 2.8: Prediction error subject to the number of training queries and the training algorithm

Figure 2.8a shows the prediction error depending on the number of queries during training for the different training algorithms. From a training phase of 70 queries, the prediction error is acceptable for each of the training algorithms, and does not change significantly anymore. *MinComb* and its variations *MinCombMaxUnknown* and *MinCombMinUnknown* perform best, *FIFO* lies in the middle field, and *MinUnknown* and *MaxUnknown* achieve the worst results. *MinCombMaxUnknown* and *MinCombMinUnknown* both quickly reach a small prediction error after only about 30 training queries while *MinComb* results in the greatest prediction error of all training algorithms with such a training length. When considering the net prediction error shown in Figure 2.8b, the reason for this becomes obvious. *MinComb* has the smallest net prediction error while the net prediction error of *MinCombMaxUnknown* and *MinCombMinUnknown* is almost equal to the prediction error. Thus, the bad overall prediction error performance of *MinComb* follows from empty synergy matrix fields, which of course result in a high error coefficient for the combinations containing the respective query pairs. The results in Figure 2.8a prove that the intended goal of the strategies *MinCombMaxUnknown* and *MinCombMinUnknown* to combine the strengths of *MinComb* and *MaxUnknown*, or *MinComb* and *MinUnknown*, respectively, is achieved. The prediction error for these strategies is close to the minimum of their base strategies. The behavior of *FIFO* is as expected, because as many good combinations (i.e., combinations that provide important information for the synergy matrix) as bad combinations (i.e., always the same combinations not serving for new information) may be selected by chance, thus resulting in a middle-rate performance. Also the prediction error of *MaxUnknown* is not surprising as this strategy quickly fills the synergy matrix with (unprecise) values, but does not effectively try to improve the values after that. The bad performance of *MinUnknown* compared to *MinCombMinUnknown* with regard to both the prediction error and the net prediction error can be explained by having a look at the implementation of those algorithms. Both of them prefer combinations with the least unknown variables, however, the first criterion of *MinCombMinUnknown* is the number of occurrences for the different combinations, which are examined in a sorted order. Therefore, it is more likely that those combinations are selected which not only provide a precise new value but at the same time also provide new information for the already known variables. This improves the precision of the synergy matrix in total.

The comparison of Figures 2.8a and 2.8b also confirms another expectation. With five query types and the MPL being set to three, there are 35 different combinations of queries (10 with different query types, 20 with two queries of the same type, and 5 with all three queries of the same type), resulting in equations with 3 (different query types), 2 (two queries of the same type), or 1 (all three queries of the same type) possibly unknown values of shares. Therefore, we expect the synergy matrix to be filled after a training phase of $10 \cdot 3 + 20 \cdot 2 + 5 \cdot 1 = 75$ queries. As the graphs in Figures 2.8a and 2.8b are quite equal for training phases of this length or longer, i.e., the net prediction error does not differ from the prediction error because of empty synergy matrix fields, our expectation is met.

The response times of combinations executed in a database is subject to fluctuations due to external processes reserving system resources or the database buffer containing required data or not at the time the queries are executed. In order to quantify the influence of such fluctuations on the training algorithms, we extended the simulation to enable uniformly distributed execution time fluctuations in an $\pm \varepsilon$ interval around the real value. Figure 2.9a shows the relative prediction error of the training phase with $\varepsilon = 30\%$. Compared to the execution without fluctuations shown in Figure 2.8a, the prediction error increases only slightly. The same holds for the net prediction error shown in Figure 2.9b. By repeated execution of the query combinations and computation of the average of the measured response times, fluctuations are compensated within the synergy computation over time.

The strategy *MinCombMaxUnknown* shows the best balanced behavior regarding the precision and the fast filling of the synergy matrix. We therefore use it in the following evaluation of the optimization phase.

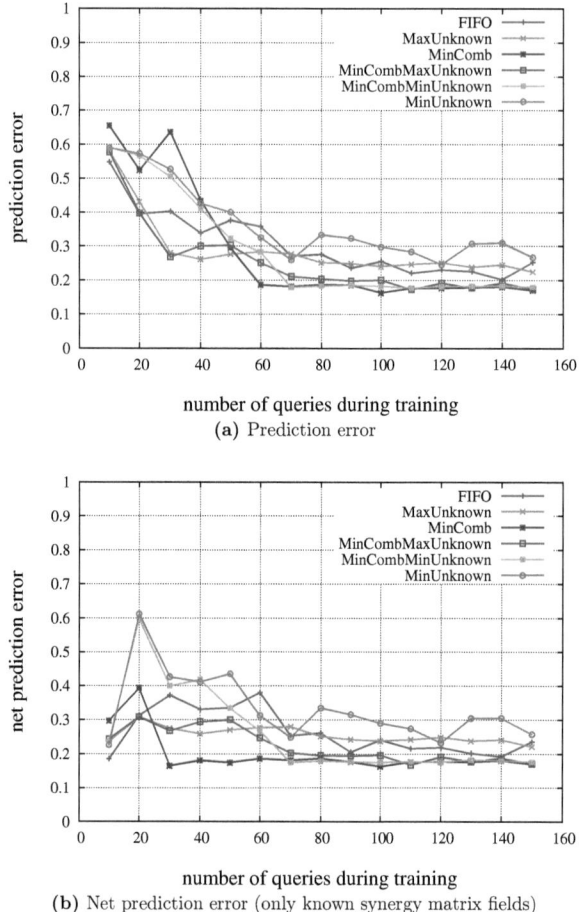

(a) Prediction error

(b) Net prediction error (only known synergy matrix fields)

Figure 2.9: Prediction error subject to the number of training queries and the training algorithm with a simulated execution time deviation of 30%

2.5.4 Optimization Phase

The primary goal of the optimization phase is to minimize the execution time of all waiting queries. In order to achieve comparable results, we chose a batch scenario for the evaluation where all queries are queued at the beginning of the optimization phase. Thus, no deviations due to different arrival times of queries can occur as it is the case for interactive workloads.

We analyze the optimization phase with respect to the effect of synergy exploitation and the importance of accurate synergy values in Figure 2.10. First, we compare the total execution times of workloads of varying sizes using *FIFO* scheduling and the *MaxSyn*

2.5 Simulation

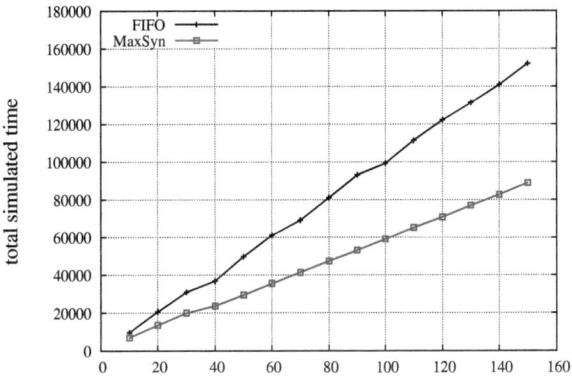

(a) Comparison of workload execution times using *FIFO* and *MaxSyn* scheduling (based on the synergy matrix built from a training workload of 50 queries) in the optimization phase

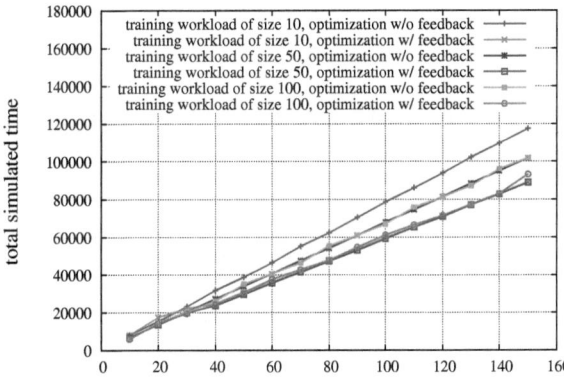

(b) Effect of short vs. long training phase and feedback in the optimization phase

Figure 2.10: Effect of synergy exploitation and feedback during the optimization phase

scheduling algorithm based on synergies. The result is shown in Figure 2.10a. The larger the workload, the more significant is a good scheduling to achieve a short workload execution time. The unoptimized execution of a workload containing 150 queries using *FIFO* takes almost twice as long as the optimized execution with a preceding training phase of 50 queries and continuous feedback of execution time information into the synergy computation. We then examine the impact of the training phase duration on the accuracy and completeness of the computed synergy values. Figure 2.10b shows the total execution times for the execution of workloads of different sizes with and without feedback during the optimization phase. We compare the processing times using the *MaxSyn* strategy with

Approach	Type of synergy		
	Resource-based	Data-based	Query-based
Scan-sharing	✓	✓✓✓	✓
Request window	✓✓	✓✓✓	✓
Caching	✓✓✓	✓✓	✓
Intermediate results	✓	✓	✓✓✓
Plan-caching	✓✓✓		✓
Common subexpression	✓✓✓	✓	✓✓

Table 2.3: Approaches to exploit sources of synergies (adapted from Wylezich (2011))

a preceding training phase of 10, 50, and 100 queries. A longer training phase results in more useful synergy values, however, the synergy matrix seems to be sufficiently filled after a training phase of 50 queries. Without feedback in the optimization phase, the performance decrease for a workload of 150 queries is 20% for a short training phase of 10 queries compared to a longer one with 50 queries. If, by contrast, the information gathered during the optimization phase is fed back into the synergy computation, the execution times of the workloads with short and long training phases do not differ significantly. The feedback thus has a considerable effect on the total workload performance.

2.6 Synergies in State-of-the-Art Database Systems

Sources of synergy are on one hand naturally given by the underlying hardware of a database system, e.g., the available number of cores and their clock rate or the maximum throughput of the disks, and the resulting contention. On the other hand, database systems implement a multitude of features ranging from simple caching to complex multi-query optimization, which create new sources of synergy.

Table 2.3 gives an overview of approaches to exploit sources of synergies. Typically, the approaches do not fall exactly into one of the identified categories (resource-based, data-based, or query-based), rather there are overlaps between the categories. We therefore indicate how far the respective approach takes advantage of the respective sources of synergies by assigning 0 to 3 points to each category.

Scan-sharing lets a second query on the same base table participate in an already started table scan. After the shared scan is finished, the second query scans the rest of the data. The approach has been described by Lang et al. (2007) and Zukowski et al. (2007) and is implemented in IBM DB2 V9.7 and in the Microsoft SQL Server 2000 Enterprise Edition. Request windows are similar but they queue requests for a certain time window in order to combine them to a single query. The result is then partitioned again into the result sets of the original queries. For this approach, it is crucial to determine the maximal time window as shown by Lee et al. (2007). Caching reduces the number of expensive disk accesses and enables data sharing. It is exploited by most database systems. Intermediate results can be cached for a certain time, so they don't have to be re-computed for repeated occurrences of the same queries. The MonetDB Recycler implements this approach. Plan-caching refers to storing parameterized execution plans, thus saving costly optimizations for subsequent queries of the same type. The Microsoft SQL Server supports plan-caching.

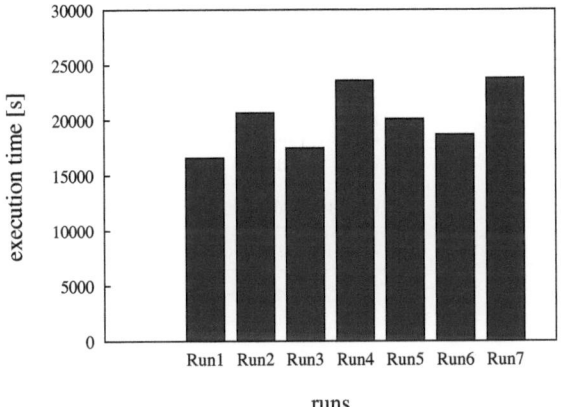

Figure 2.11: Execution time of different TPC-H-based workload schedules (runs) on DBMS-X (adapted from Wylezich (2011))

Common subexpressions are redundant parts of execution plans on both inter- and intra-query level. They can be exploited to optimize globally over a multitude of queries, not locally for a single query. Dalvi et al. (2003) and Roy et al. (2000) investigate algorithms for determining and making use of common subexpressions.

We focus on the scan-sharing feature of a commercial database system, called DBMS-X in the following, in order to verify our findings based on the simulation framework for real database systems and real workloads. The benchmark results we employ in our analysis are taken from the Master's Thesis of Wylezich (2011), which was supervised by the author of this thesis. The tested database system is running on a Linux server with 8 GB of RAM. The database is created using the publicly available TPC-H data generator with a scale factor of 50 resulting in about 50 GB of data. The database size is chosen such that caching effects cannot be exploited. The complete benchmark settings can be taken from Wylezich (2011). The workload consists of five instances of each of the TPC-H queries $Q1$, $Q2$, $Q3$, $Q4$, $Q9$, and $Q13$, which execute table and index scans on the largest TPC-H tables `Lineitem` and `Orders`. They exhibit different CPU and I/O usage characteristics and scan speeds, and allow for an effective analysis of the scan-sharing effects depending on the queries' properties. The benchmarks are conducted using an MPL of 5.

Figure 2.11 shows the execution times of seven different schedules of the workload, called runs. The execution time difference between the fastest (Run1) and the slowest (Run7) schedule is about 44%. It becomes evident that scheduling has a high impact on the execution time of the workload.

We fed the execution times measured by Wylezich (2011) for the different combinations of the runs[2] into the synergy computation and computed the values given in Figure 2.12. The synergies between different pairs of query types differ significantly. For instance, $Q13$ and $Q9$ have a high negative synergy. This is because they operate on different tables

---

[2] We used the monitored values with a standard deviation for one combination smaller than 20% as the total size of the workload was too small for the synergy computation to react to outliers.

$Q1$	-111	-107	309	91	84	42
$Q2$	5	0	-45	102	-285	219
$Q9$	514	48	402	318	-288	-481
$Q3$	-12	-113	10	71	206	41
$Q4$	172	-309	-405	397	366	172
$Q13$	62	127	-666	164	104	208
q_1/q_2	$Q1$	$Q2$	$Q9$	$Q3$	$Q4$	$Q13$

Figure 2.12: Synergy values for the TPC-H queries $Q1$, $Q2$, $Q9$, $Q3$, $Q4$, and $Q13$ on DBMS-X

and thus cannot profit from scan-sharing. On the other hand, $Q9$ has a high positive synergy with $Q1$ as they both scan the Lineitem table. Some of the synergy values are hard to explain as besides scan-sharing, also the contention of queries for resources has a high impact on the overall execution times of query sets. Wylezich (2011) analyzed the workload runs with respect to different measures like number of disk accesses, CPU utilization, throttling time, etc., but could not find considerable correlations between one of these measures and the execution times of the runs. However, the comparison of the ranking of execution times and synergy values in Table 2.4 confirms that there is a high correlation between these two.

Ranking	Execution time [s]		Synergy	
1.	Run1	16592	Run1	18720
2.	Run3	17486	Run3	18208
3.	Run6	18699	Run6	16800
4.	Run5	20124	Run5	8432
5.	Run2	20664	Run7	6960
6.	Run4	23627	Run2	5734
7.	Run7	23813	Run4	3152

Table 2.4: Correlation between synergy values and execution times of different TPC-H workload schedules

The synergy values allow to clearly separate the efficient (fast) schedules of the workload from the inefficient (slow). Although the synergy values cannot be directly mapped to execution times, from the comparison above we are confident that they are expressive enough to enable scheduling the workload such that the synergies created by DBMS-X are exploited.

2.7 Summary and Conclusions

The efficient scheduling of database workloads is an intensely researched field in the context of workload management. However, most of the developed approaches focus on only one source of synergy, thereby ignoring the potential influences of other synergy factors. Other approaches are not applicable at runtime as they require a preceding offline phase in order to gather information.

We developed a monitoring-based approach for the optimization of database workloads, which collects synergy information and flexibly integrates new query types at runtime. By using the execution time of query combinations as an indicator for synergies, we concentrate on optimizing the ultimate goal of scheduling and at the same time do not run the risk of ignoring any sources of synergy with an effect on workload performance. Our approach is completely independent of the underlying system's hardware or the database system used. Furthermore, it is transparent to the client and the database system. This is achieved by designing the optimization component as a middleware layer between these two. By dividing the monitored execution times of query sets into pairwise shares and by solving the resulting linear equation system, we derive synergies between queries. In a training phase, we execute different combinations of queries in order to gain broad knowledge of existing synergies and to avoid optimizing for local maxima. Subsequently, we exploit the detected synergies in an optimization phase to efficiently process database queries. The monitored execution times are fed back into synergy computation. Training and optimization phases can be switched as required. This allows for completing and enhancing synergy information in training mode in times of low load on the database system. When system load is high, system performance is improved by scheduling based on synergies in optimization mode.

Using a simulation framework, we compared different scheduling algorithms for the training phase with respect to their ability to fill the synergy matrix quickly and with precise values. For this purpose, we defined a quality measure called prediction error, which represents the deviation of estimated execution times based on the computed shares from real execution times over all combinations. We found that a strategy aiming at quickly filling all synergy matrix fields achieves the best results (Figure 2.8). We further verified the effectivity of synergy-based scheduling in the optimization phase. For a workload consisting of 150 queries, the optimized scheduling according to the detected synergies improves the total execution time by almost a factor of two compared to an unoptimized scheduling according to query arrival (Figure 2.10a). We also examined the benefit of feeding back monitoring information into the synergy computation during the optimization phase and found that enabling this feedback loop is even preferable over a long training phase (Figure 2.10b).

Today's database systems offer a multitude of features ranging from simple caching to complex multi-query optimization. These features create sources of synergy, which can be exploited using our approach. We showed this for the scan-sharing feature of a commercial database system. For a workload consisting of 30 TPC-H queries, we examined seven exemplary schedules, of which the total execution times vary up to 44%. A comparison of workload execution times and synergy values confirms that there is a high correlation between these two measurements (Table 2.4).

Chapter 3

Robust Query Execution – The Generalized Join Algorithm

Scalable analytical query processing presumes a certain predictability of query execution behavior in order to effectively allocate resources to different transactional and analytical workloads submitted to the database. For query execution to be predictable, each of the query's execution plan operators needs to perform in a calculable way. We focus on the relational join, the probably most important database operator. There exist a lot of physical implementations of the logical join operator, which differ in execution time, memory consumption, and preferred inputs. Traditional database query processing relies on three types of algorithms for join operations based on hashing, sorting, and indexes, respectively. Physical data independence and the declarative nature of SQL require query optimization to choose the most appropriate algorithm based on the estimated query execution costs. Unfortunately, mistaken algorithm choices during compile-time query optimization are common yet expensive to investigate and to resolve.

Generalized join (g-join) has been proposed by Graefe (2012) as a new join algorithm replacing the traditional algorithms and thus eliminating the need for (possibly wrong) optimizer decisions. Specifically, it addresses the problem of algorithm choices. In this chapter, we present the g-join algorithm and explain it by means of an extensive example. We then address design alternatives and our implementation of g-join within the query processing system HyPer/dbcore in detail. Furthermore, we give an overview of the implementations of hash join, sort-merge join, and index nested-loops join in HyPer/dbcore before we provide the results of a detailed comparative evaluation of the presented algorithms. These substantiate earlier claims by Graefe (2012) about robust query execution time and memory consumption. We finally go beyond join computation and depict the adaptation of the g-join concept to aggregation and duplicate removal operations.

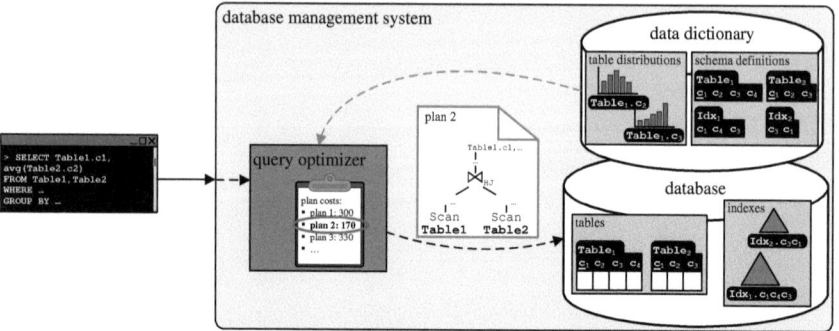

Figure 3.1: Query processing in a relational database management system: a user submits a request to the database management system, the optimizer generates an efficient execution plan for it by calculating the costs for a multitude of alternative plans and by choosing the cheapest, which is then executed on the database tables and indexes

3.1 Introduction

Query processing in relational database management systems is basically structured as sketched in Figure 3.1: Users submit requests to the database system, the query optimizer determines efficient execution plans for the requests, and the plans are then run against the database. A request is typically expressed using a declarative query language like SQL. Within the database system, it is initially translated to a normalized execution plan consisting of cross products followed by a selection and a projection operator. The query optimizer then transforms this correct but inefficient plan to an equivalent and efficient execution plan consisting of table and index scans, selections, joins, and other operations. Finally, the plan is executed on the base tables and indexes as indicated. A cost-based query optimizer enumerates a multitude of equivalent query execution plans by varying data access paths, join orders, selection placements, operator implementations, and many more, computes the estimated costs for each plan on the basis of known or estimated factors either given by the request itself or stored in the data dictionary, and returns the least-cost plan. Of course, the quality of the resulting execution plan heavily depends on the correctness and accuracy of the information that the query optimizer uses to compute the plan costs. In Table 3.1, we list the most common query optimizer inputs and classify them by their type (quantitative or qualitative) and accuracy (knowledge or estimate). Quantitative information, e.g., cardinalities of tables or indexes and selectivities of operators, is almost always taken from statistics, which may not be up to date or heavily compressed. Only when an intermediate result is computed by executing an exact match selection on a primary key or in the case of a primary key – foreign key join (assuming referential integrity), quantitative information is definitely precise. However, in general, this kind of information is not reliable. By contrast, qualitative information, e.g., whether or not inputs to an operator are sorted, usually stems from given facts, e.g., a previous sort operator or a sorted data structure such as a B-tree[3], and are thus reliable.

---

[3]We assume sorted persistent indexes throughout the chapter.

3.1 Introduction

Input	Type		Accuracy	
	Quantitative	Qualitative	Knowledge	Estimate
Table cardinalities	✓			✓
Index cardinalities	✓			✓
Intermediate result cardinalities	✓		✓	✓
Value distributions	✓			✓
Input sort orders		✓	✓	
Join selectivities	✓		✓	✓
Existing indexes		✓	✓	

Table 3.1: Classification of inputs to a query optimizer

One of the decisions the optimizer has to make based on the given information is which physical join implementation is the best to realize a logical join in the execution plan. Traditional physical join implementations are hash-based, sort-based, or index-based. Sort-based joins take advantage of sorted inputs, e.g., in case they can either be read sorted from an index or are sorted by a prior operator. Hash-based join algorithms are favorable if one of the inputs is very small or even fits in main memory. The preprocessing before the actual join phase depends mainly on the smaller of the two inputs. Index-based join algorithms make use of available persistent indexes for one input (called the inner input) to efficiently find join partners and are best if the outer input is fairly small or sorted. Depending on the qualitative and quantitative information the optimizer is provided, it heuristically calculates costs for alternative execution plans including either hash-based, sort-based, or index-based joins. However, it is not uncommon that heuristics are poor and statistics are not up to date and this results in mistaken algorithm choices and bad query execution performance.

Graefe (2012) proposed a new join algorithm called generalized join (g-join) to replace the traditional algorithms and thus eliminate the need for (possibly wrong) optimizer decisions. G-join combines the advantages of sort-merge join (exploits and roughly preserves interesting orders), hash join (exploits different input sizes and fast probing for join partners), and index nested-loops join (exploits existent indexes). As opposed to traditional join algorithms, the performance of g-join does not depend on the accuracy of statistics. However, qualitative information like whether an input is sorted, is applied. Table 3.2 summarizes the input characteristics exploited by index nested-loops join (INLJ), sort-merge join (SMJ), hash join (HJ), and the new g-join (GJ).

	INLJ	SMJ	HJ	GJ
Indexed input(s)	✓			✓
Sorted input(s)		✓		✓
Size difference			✓	✓

Table 3.2: Join algorithms and the input properties they exploit (adapted from Graefe (2012))

G-join for unsorted, unindexed inputs starts by sorting the join arguments to form initial runs but it omits the merge step that generates the total order. Rather, it moves synchronously through all runs of both inputs. The active runs of the (smaller) left input are combined in an in-memory index, which is probed page by page of the runs from the (larger) right input. Unlike hash join, there is no (clear) separation between build and probe phase. Instead, the probe mechanism continuously (at page boundaries) triggers eviction of a page from and loading of a new page into the in-memory index. G-join is a hybrid of sort-merge join and hash join and in some cases also inherits advantages of index nested-loops join:

- Like hash join, g-join exploits two inputs of different sizes by building the in-memory index for the smaller of the two join inputs.
- Like sort-merge join, g-join takes advantage of prior sort orders and generates nearly sorted output, which can be exploited in complex query plans as shown by Selinger et al. (1979).
- Like index nested-loops join, g-join makes use of available persistent indexes on relevant attributes for the build input instead of maintaining a temporary in-memory index.

We integrated g-join into the modern main-memory-centric database system HyPer by Kemper and Neumann (2011). Even though HyPer is a main memory database system that retains the entire transactional database in RAM, the query processor spools intermediate results to disk to preserve the precious RAM capacity for the transactional working set. Therefore, the entire spectrum of g-join is exploited in HyPer, ranging from a pure main memory algorithm to a hybrid g-join spilling some of its inputs from memory, and to an entirely disk-based processing mode with a very small RAM footprint. This is the first complete implementation of g-join extending preliminary insights gained by an initial prototype of Li (2010).

3.2 Basic Algorithm

Before going into detail with respect to implementation alternatives and different kinds of inputs, we will first address the general case of unsorted, unindexed, large inputs and adhere to the implementation suggestions given by Graefe (2012).

G-join basically works in two phases as sketched in Algorithm 3.1: (1) a run generation phase and (2) a join phase. The phases share characteristics of the partitioning and join phases of hash join and of the sort and join phases of sort-merge join. In the first phase, g-join generates sorted runs from its inputs like sort-merge join, but avoids to merge them if memory requirements allow for it. The concrete conditions under which a merge phase can be omitted are explained in detail in Graefe (2012). In the second phase, g-join traverses the left and right input runs synchronously and brings together matching tuples by use of an in-memory index structure. Thereby, at any time, g-join requires on average two pages of each left input run and one page of the right input to be in memory. G-join further maintains priority queues to guide the loading of left input pages into and the removing of the pages from the buffer pool and to determine the next page of the right input to be processed.

3.2 Basic Algorithm

Algorithm 3.1: g-join for unsorted and unindexed inputs larger than memory

Data: input relations R and S
/* first phase: run generation   */
1 generate N_R sorted runs $R_i, 1 \leq i \leq N_R$;
2 generate N_S sorted runs $S_i, 1 \leq i \leq N_S$;
   /* initialize data structures for join phase   */
3 create in-memory index;
4 **foreach** $R_i, 1 \leq i \leq N_R$ **do**
5   load first page p_{i1} of R_i into buffer pool;
6   iterate through all entries of p_{i1} and insert them into in-memory index;
7      $max_i \leftarrow$ maximum value on p_{i1};
8 **end**
   /* each entry in priority queues A, B, and C is a pair of sort (join) key sk and run identifier rid */
9 initialize priority queues A and B with N_R entries $sk{=}max_i$, $rid{=}i$, $1 \leq i \leq N_R$;
10 **foreach** $S_i, 1 \leq i \leq N_S$ **do**
11     $min_i \leftarrow$ minimum value on first page of S_i;
12 **end**
13 initialize priority queue C with N_S entries $sk{=}min_i$, $rid{=}i$, $1 \leq i \leq N_S$;
   /* second phase: join   */
14 **while** C *is not empty* **do**
       /* determine page to be processed next   */
15     $id \leftarrow C.top().rid$;
16     $p \leftarrow$ next page of run S_{id};
17   **if** p *is NULL* **then**
           /* run S_{id} finished   */
18   remove entry for S_{id} from priority queue C;
19   **else**
20   process-page(p);   /* Algorithm 3.2 */
21   **end**
22 **end**

3.2.1 Overview

Figure 3.2 illustrates the core algorithm of g-join during the join phase.[4] Various pages (double-ended lines) from various runs cover some sub-ranges of the domain of join key values (dotted horizontal arrow). The minimum and maximum values for most of the pages are specified on the lines, some were left out for ease of presentation but can be seen in the extended example in Figure 3.4a. Some pages of runs from input R are resident in the buffer pool (solid lines), whereas some pages have already been expelled or not yet been loaded (dotted lines). The left input pages in the buffer pool determine the **immediate join key range** (shaded box), which is defined as the intersection of the buffer-pool-resident key ranges of all runs from input R. The box is delimited by a zigzag line at the left side, which stands for the left open interval starting at $-\infty$ at the beginning of the join phase.[5] As indicated by the shaded arrow, the immediate join key range moves synchronously across the runs so that join processing follows roughly the sort order of the join key values. Pages with higher key values successively replace pages

---

[4]Large parts of the following description are taken from Graefe (2012).

[5]The intersection of join key intervals on left input pages cannot contain values smaller than any key on those pages. However, right input tuples having smaller join keys can be processed (and won't find a join partner). Thus, the immediate join key range formally starts at $-\infty$ before any left input pages have been evicted from the buffer pool.

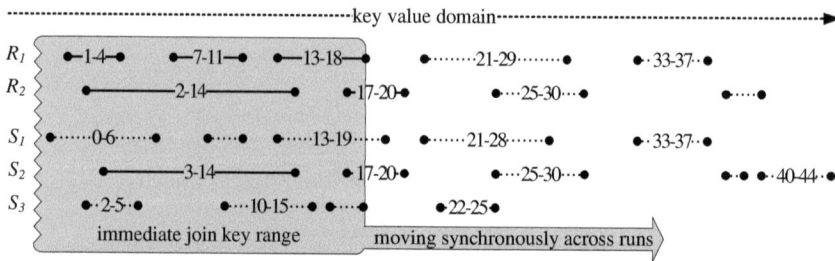

Figure 3.2: Runs R_i and S_j with key ranges per page: buffer-pool-resident pages ●—● of R_i form the immediate join key range with which one page of S_j is joined; the other pages ●⋯● have already been processed and discarded or have not been loaded yet (state snapshot of processing step 3 in Figure 3.4a)

with lower key values in the buffer pool. Some pages of runs from input S are covered by the immediate join key range, whereas some have already been joined or cannot be joined yet. At any time, memory holds multiple pages of each run from input R but only one page of one of the runs from input S (solid line). Thus, even if there are many more runs from input S than from input R, the memory requirements do not change. The snapshot in Figure 3.2 corresponds to join processing step 3 of the example shown in Figure 3.4a and discussed in Section 3.2.3: The buffer pool contains three pages of run R_1 and two of run R_2 and the first page of run S_2, which is currently being joined with the R pages in the buffer pool.

3.2.2 Data Structures and Page Processing

The immediate join key range expands and contracts as it moves from left to right through the domain. Multiple priority queues guide the schedule of page movements. In detail, our g-join implementation maintains the following three priority queues (the original g-join paper describes a fourth optional priority queue D, which we did not implement):

- Priority queue A guides loading left input pages into the buffer pool. There is one entry for each left input run. The sort key is the highest key of the run loaded so far. The top entry is the entry with the lowest sort key and indicates the run from which the next page should be loaded. That way, the immediate join key range is (most probably) effectively extended with each newly loaded page, thus minimizing the risk of filling the buffer pool with data without making use of it.

- Priority queue B guides removing left input pages from the buffer pool. There is one entry for each left input run. The sort key is the highest key on the oldest page of the run in the buffer pool. The top entry is the entry with the lowest sort key and indicates the run from which the oldest page should be removed. This makes sure that the immediate join key range shrinks stepwise, thereby enabling to eliminate pages from the buffer pool early, while still keeping the immediate join key range large enough to process the probe input.

- Priority queue C guides processing right input pages. There is one entry for each right input run. The sort key is the highest key of the run processed so far. The

3.2 Basic Algorithm

Algorithm 3.2: process-page of right input run during join phase

Data: page p of right input run S_{cur} to be processed
/* each entry in priority queues A, B, and C is a pair of sort (join) key sk and run identifier rid */
/* remove data from in-memory index and buffer pool */
1. **while** $B.top().sk < C.top().sk$ **do**
2. $id \leftarrow B.top().rid$;
3. $r \leftarrow$ oldest page of R_{id} in buffer pool;
4.   iterate through all entries of r and remove from in-memory index;
5.   remove r from buffer pool;
6. $r' \leftarrow$ (new) oldest page of R_{id} in buffer pool;
7. $max_{r'} \leftarrow$ maximum entry on r';
8.   update priority queue B with $sk=max_{r'}$, $rid=id$;
9. **end**
 /* load data into in-memory index and buffer pool if key range on p is not covered by the immediate join key range */
10. $max \leftarrow$ maximum entry on p;
11. **while** $A.top().sk \leq max$ **do**
12. $id \leftarrow A.top().rid$;
13. $i \leftarrow$ next page to read of R_{id};
14.   iterate through all entries of i and insert into in-memory index;
15. $max_i \leftarrow$ maximum entry on i;
16.   update priority queue A with $sk=max_i$, $rid=id$;
17. **end**
 /* process current page of the right input */
18. **foreach** *entry e on p* **do**
19.   probe into in-memory index using e;
20.   **if** *match found* **then**
21.   produce join result;
22.   **end**
23. **end**
24. update priority queue C with $sk=max$, $rid=cur$;

---

top entry is the entry with the lowest sort key and indicates the run from which the next page should be processed. That way, the probe input is processed page by page in join key order which produces a roughly sorted output.

When the priority queues are initialized, the entries in A and B are the same as initially the first page of each left input run is loaded into the buffer pool. The entries in priority queue C are initialized with the minimum value on the first page of each run from the right input.

During the join phase, pages from the right input are processed one by one as described in Algorithm 3.2. Priority queue C determines the order in which pages are processed. For each page of the right input, the in-memory index is updated as needed, i.e., old entries are removed if they are no longer needed and new entries are inserted. Priority queues B and A guide removing and inserting and are updated accordingly. Then, the index is probed with each value in the page and result tuples are generated. After each entry on the page has been processed, priority queue C is updated with the maximum (last) value processed.

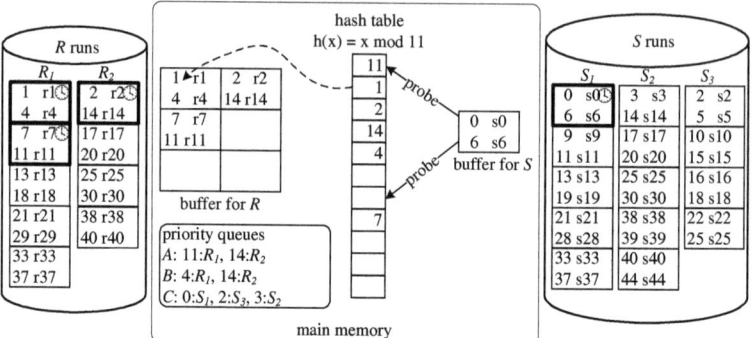

(a) Processing the 1st page of S_1 ($C.top().rid=S_1$): pages from input R are initially loaded into the buffer pool and references to their data are inserted into the hash table until the immediate join key range allows processing the current page, i.e., $[0,6] \subset \ ]-\infty,11[$

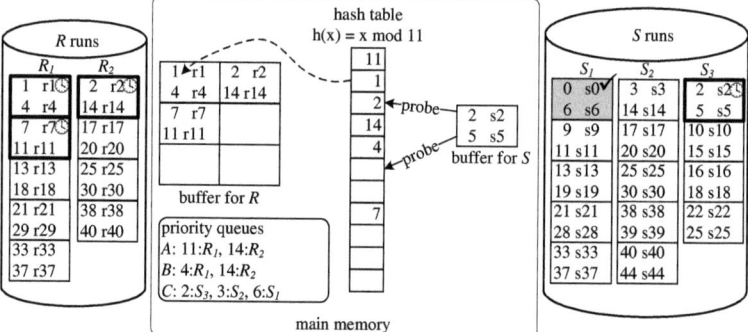

(b) Processing the 1st page of S_3 ($C.top().rid=S_3$): no hash table update necessary as the immediate join key range allows processing the current page, i.e., $[2,5] \subset \ ]-\infty,11[$

Figure 3.3: G-join example: join phase

3.2.3 Example

Figures 3.3 and 3.4 illustrate how g-join loads pages into and removes pages from the buffer pool and how the data structures are updated. As proposed by Graefe (2012), we use a hash table as in-memory index structure in the example. Let R_1, R_2, S_1, S_2, and S_3 denote the runs of R and S, respectively, after run generation. For ease of presentation, each page (rectangles in the figure) contains only two records. Each record consists of the join key (= sort key) and payload data, of which the values are preceded by "r" or "s", respectively. For the left input, we provide six buffer pool frames, for the right input only one buffer pool frame is required during the join phase. Throughout the example, the currently processed (and buffer-pool-resident) pages are framed thickly and marked by a clock in the upper right corner. Pages that have been processed completely and will not be read again are shaded and labeled with a check mark in the upper right corner.

3.2 Basic Algorithm

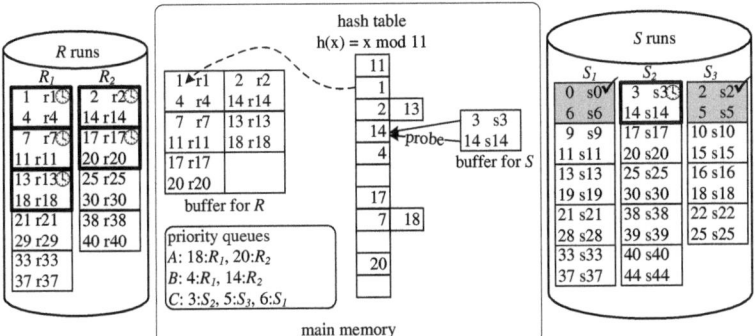

(a) Processing the 1st page of S_2 ($C.top().rid=S_2$): pages from input R are loaded into the buffer pool and references to their data are inserted into the hash table until the immediate join key range allows processing the current page, i.e., $[3,14] \subset]-\infty,18[$.

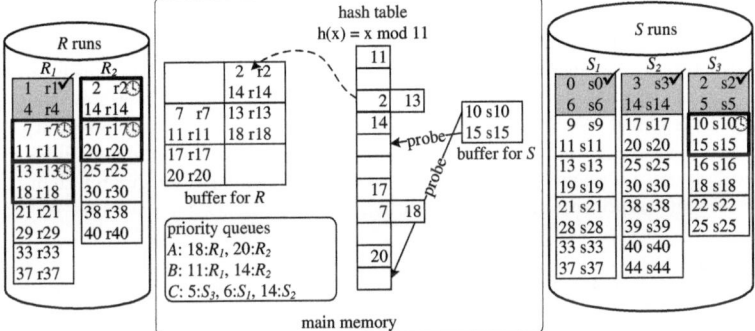

(b) Processing the 2nd page of S_3 ($C.top().rid=S_3$): pages from input R are unloaded from the buffer pool and their references are removed from the hash table as long as the immediate join key range still allows processing the current page, i.e., $[10,15] \subset]7,18[$.

Figure 3.4: G-join example: join phase (cont'd)

The priority queues hold one entry per run of the respective input, i.e., priority queues A and B have two entries referring to R_1 and R_2 each, priority queue C has three entries referring to S_1, S_2, and S_3. One priority queue entry consists of a sort key and a run identifier, e.g., $11:R_1$.

Figure 3.3a shows the state of the buffer pool and the hash table when the first page of input S is processed: The first two pages of R_1 and the first page of R_2 are resident in the buffer pool. While the first page of each R run is initially loaded into the hash table at the beginning of the join phase, loading of the second page of R_1 is triggered by the join key range on the first S page to be processed. For each tuple on the loaded R pages, an entry consisting of the tuple's join key and a reference to its memory location (dashed arrow) is inserted into the hash table. For ease of presentation, only one reference from an entry in the hash table to an actual page in the buffer pool is shown. The immediate join key range is $]-\infty,11[$. Note that the interval is open to the right. This is because there might be duplicates of 11 on future pages of R_1 and thus this join key cannot be processed at the moment. The entries of priority queue A denote the highest keys loaded so far (11 for run R_1 and 14 for run R_2) and the entries of priority queue B hold the highest keys on the oldest pages of each run in the buffer pool (4 for run R_1 and again 14 for run R_2 as there is only one page from this run currently in the buffer pool). The entries of priority queue C are initialized with the minimum entries on the first pages of S_1 (0), S_2 (3), and S_3 (2). These values were recorded during the prior run generation phase. As the top of priority queue C is 0:S_1, the first page of S_1 is processed first. The immediate join key range allows processing it, thus the hash table is probed for the keys 0 and 6. Subsequently, priority queue C's entry for S_1 is updated with the value 6 as shown in Figure 3.3b. In the next step, the first page of S_3 is processed. There is no need to update the hash table, we can look up the values 2 and 5 on the page and update priority queue C. The third step, i.e., the join of the first page of S_2 shown in Figure 3.4a requires a hash table update. According to priority queue A, the third page of R_1 is loaded into the buffer pool. At first glance, this appears to be sufficient. However, the immediate join key range at this moment is $]-\infty,14[$ and thus does not contain 14. Therefore, the second page of R_2 is also loaded into the buffer pool and the respective entries are inserted into the hash table. As illustrated, collisions in the hash table are handled using chaining. After processing the current page, priority queue C is updated. In step four, the second page of S_3 is joined. No data from R needs to be loaded into the buffer pool but the first page of R_1 (to which the top entry of priority queue B points) containing the key value range $[1,4]$ can be removed as future join keys will be equal to or greater than the top entry sort key of priority queue C, which has the value 5.

3.3 G-Join in Detail

After having sketched the basic g-join components and data processing, we will now discuss the complete g-join algorithm in detail, including hybrid g-join, which builds the glue between pure in-memory processing and disk-based join computation. Furthermore, we present design alternatives and discuss their performance impact. We finally cover g-join for outer, semi, and anti semi joins.

3.3.1 Detailed Algorithm

In Section 3.2, we described g-join for unsorted and unindexed inputs larger than main memory. Now, we will address the strength of g-join to naturally exploit qualitative information like sort order of inputs and data structures like available indexes, which renders it competitive to the traditional join algorithms based on hashing, sorting, or indexes. Algorithm 3.3 provides the complete `g-join` algorithm, which we describe in the following.

In-Memory Execution. If one of the inputs is small enough to fit in main memory, the in-memory variant of g-join shown in Algorithm 3.4, `in-memory-join`, is called (lines 1 to 6 in Algorithm 3.3). Thereby, the main-memory-resident data is transformed to an in-memory index and probed using the second (possibly much greater) input without any preprocessing. G-join thus shares the advantage of hash join in case input sizes differ

3.3 G-Join in Detail

Algorithm 3.3: g-join complete algorithm

Data: inputs R and S, tags $sorted_R$ and $sorted_S$ specifying an existing (relevant) sort order for R and S, pointers to persistent indexes $index_R$ and $index_S$

```
   /* in-memory cases                                                  */
 1 if R fits in main memory then
 2  |  in-memory-join(R, S);                            /* Algorithm 3.4 */
 3 end
 4 if S fits in main memory then
 5  |  in-memory-join(S, R);                            /* Algorithm 3.4 */
 6 end
   /* on-disk cases                                                     */
 7 buildInput ← 0;
 8 probeInput ← 0;
   /* run generation                                                    */
 9 if ¬sorted_R ∧ ¬index_R then
      /* generate N_R sorted runs R_i, 1 ≤ i ≤ N_R                      */
10   |  N_R ← run-generation(R);
11 end
12 if ¬sorted_S ∧ ¬index_S then
      /* generate N_S sorted runs S_i, 1 ≤ i ≤ N_S                      */
13   |  N_S ← run-generation(S);
14 end
   /* assign build and probe input roles                                */
15 assign-roles(R, S, sorted_R, sorted_S, index_R, index_S, N_R, N_s); ; /* Algorithm 3.5 */
   /* join phase                                                        */
16 join(buildInput, probeInput);                        /* Algorithm 3.6 */
```

Algorithm 3.4: in-memory-join for $buildInput \leq$ available main memory

Data: two pointers to $buildInput$ and $probeInput$
```
1 build in-memory index I from buildInput;
2 foreach t ∈ probeInput do
3   |  probe into I using t;
4   |  if join partner found then
5   |   |  produce output tuple;
6   |  end
7 end
```

greatly as the efficient in-memory execution of the join depends only on the size of the smaller input. Please note that without any knowledge about input sizes, sorted runs may be generated in vain for the larger of the two inputs if it is processed first. However, statistical information is usually reliable in determining the smaller of two inputs and thus can be employed to decide on the order in which inputs are processed during run generation.

On-Disk Execution. If both inputs are larger than main memory and are neither sorted nor indexed, sorted runs are generated (lines 9 to 14 in Algorithm 3.3). We will cover the implementation of **run-generation** in detail shortly. For sorted inputs, this step is omitted. An index on the relevant columns of an input can both serve as index structure or as sorted data source and thus obviates the need for run generation. Then, the build and probe input roles are assigned to the inputs depending on their characteristics (line 15 in Algorithm 3.3) as detailed in Algorithm 3.5, **assign-roles**. Here, qualitative information

Algorithm 3.5: `assign-roles` assigns build and probe input roles to inputs

Data: inputs R and S, tags $sorted_R$ and $sorted_S$ specifying an existing (relevant) sort order for R and S, pointers to persistent indexes $index_R$ and $index_S$, integers N_R and N_S specifying the number of runs generated for R and S, respectively

```
    /* consider characteristics of input R                              */
 1  if indexR then
        /* R is indexed, consider characteristics of input S            */
 2      if indexS then                          /* role reversal if required */
 3          buildInput ← input with larger index;
 4          probeInput ← input with smaller index;
 5      end
 6      else if sortedS then
 7          buildInput ← R;
 8          probeInput ← S;
 9      end
10      else
11          buildInput ← R;
12          probeInput ← S;
13      end
14  end
15  else if sortedR then
        /* R is sorted, consider characteristics of input S             */
16      if indexS then
17          buildInput ← S;
18          probeInput ← R;
19      end
20      else if sortedS then
21          merge-join(R, S);
22      end
23      else
24          buildInput ← S;
25          probeInput ← R;
26      end
27  end
28  else
        /* R is neither indexed nor sorted, consider characteristics of input S */
29      if indexS then
30          buildInput ← S;
31          probeInput ← R;
32      end
33      else if sortedS then
34          buildInput ← R;
35          probeInput ← S;
36      end
37      else                                    /* role reversal if required */
38          Nb ← minimum of NR and NS;
39          Np ← maximum of NR and NS;
40          buildInput ← input for which fewer runs Nb were generated;
41          probeInput ← input for which more runs Np were generated;
42      end
43  end
```

3.3 G-Join in Detail

Algorithm 3.6: join phase of g-join

   Data: pointers to *buildInput* and *probeInput*
1. initialize index I using *buildInput*;
2. **while** *probeInput.next()* $\neq$ *NULL* **do**
3. $n \leftarrow$ *probeInput.next()*;
4. $I.update(n)$;
5.   probe into I using n;
6.   **if** *join partner found* **then**
7. | produce output tuple;
8.   **end**
9. **end**

---

like knowledge of given sort orders or indexes is exploited. Furthermore, knowledge about the (approximate) sizes of indexes or the number of previously generated runs is available and contributes in role reversal decisions. In particular, the algorithm proceeds as follows: The inputs are subsequently checked for given indexes or sort orders. If an index exists on the relevant attributes, it is preferred over building and maintaining a temporary in-memory index and thus it is assigned the build input role (lines 3, 7, 11, 17, and 30 in Algorithm 3.5). We experimentally evaluated that, if both inputs are indexed, it is more efficient to assign the build input role to the larger index as this incurs less index lookups. Further, sorted inputs, i.e., inputs read from a sorted index or outputs of a previous sort operator, are used as probe input because this minimizes the required immediate join key range and thus the memory consumption of g-join (lines 4, 8, 18, 25, and 35 in Algorithm 3.5). For the same reason, role reversal is considered where appropriate, i.e., the build input role is assigned to the input with smaller main memory requirements (line 37 in Algorithm 3.5). If both inputs are sorted, g-join basically resorts to merge join (line 21 in Algorithm 3.5). After build and probe input roles have been assigned, the join phase given in Algorithm 3.6 is entered. First, an index is initialized using the provided *buildInput* (line 1 in Algorithm 3.6). In case of a given permanent index, there is nothing to do, otherwise an in-memory index is instantiated. Then, the *probeInput* is processed, i.e., the index is updated as required (line 4 in Algorithm 3.6[6]) and probed, thereby producing output tuples if matches are found (lines 5 to 8 in Algorithm 3.6).

Hybrid G-join. When run generation is appropriate and the data size slightly exceeds the in-memory limit, there is an immense performance decrease compared to in-memory execution due to the disk I/O incurred by run generation and join phase. This significant overhead motivates "hybrid" join algorithms (like hybrid hash join) smoothing the execution time degradation by allowing most of the join to be computed in-memory, while a small part of the data is processed by generating intermediate data on disk. The processing resembles that of hybrid hash join as originally described by DeWitt et al. (1984).

We devise the "hybrid" g-join implementation sketched in Figure 3.5. During run generation for the left input, the low end of the join key domain is kept in a maximum heap H_{max}. When overflow occurs, the top entry[7] is spilled to the (regular) minimum heap H_{min} used for generating sorted runs. When the left input terminates, the maximum heap is reorganized as a hash table. During run generation for the right input, tuples falling

---

[6]The in-memory index update is given in more detail in Algorithm 3.2 for unindexed and unsorted inputs, for which runs have been generated.

[7]more precisely, the top entry and all its duplicates

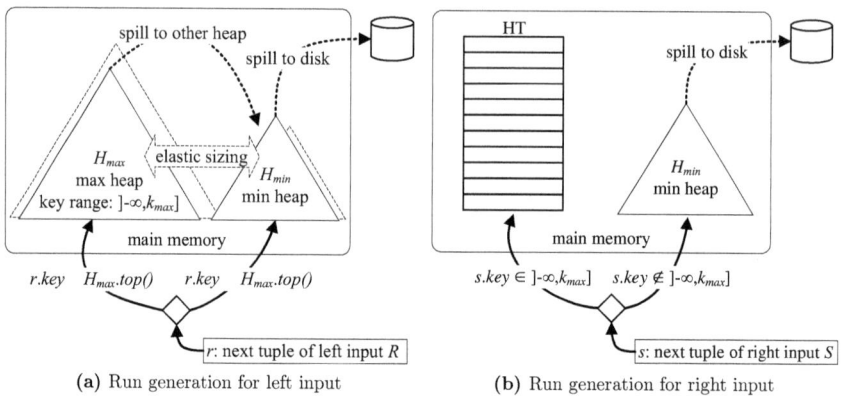

Figure 3.5: Hybrid g-join

into the key value interval $]-\infty, k_{max}]$ of the hash table are joined immediately. All other tuples are inserted into the minimum heap and participate in run generation.

Hybrid g-join initially partitions memory in favor of the maximum heap expecting the input to be only a little larger than memory if at all. As the input is processed, the size of the maximum heap is adaptively decreased to allow for a larger minimum heap resulting in longer runs. Pragmatically, we start for the first few (e.g., three) runs with 10% of the main memory for the sorting heap, increase it by 10% to 20% for the next few (three) runs, to 30% for the next few (three) runs, to 40% and 50% in the same manner. Thereafter, we give up on the hybrid variant of g-join and resort to "regular" g-join by dedicating all the RAM to run generation. The variable size of the heaps is indicated by the dashed heaps in the background in Figure 3.5a. The adaptive partitioning of memory between max and min heaps results in an effective elasticity of in-memory g-join turning over to hybrid g-join. Hybrid g-join produces first results early during run generation from the right input like the progressive sort-merge join published by Dittrich et al. (2002) and it omits writing the lowest key values to disk and re-reading them again later.

3.3.2 Design Alternatives

Although the g-join algorithm has been covered in-depth by Graefe (2011), there are still many options open for the concrete design of various components of g-join including the run generation, the in-memory index structure, and the priority queues. In the following, we shed light on the design alternatives and discuss their impact on the behavior of g-join. We further present and explain the design decisions we made in our implementation of g-join in HyPer/dbcore.

Figure 3.6 gives an overview: As described in Algorithm 3.3, g-join assigns its two inputs the roles *buildInput* and *probeInput*, which are of type *GJoinIdx* and *ProbeInput*. *GJoinIdx* represents the build input index and provides the functionality for updating (insert, remove) and querying (lookupFirst, lookupNext) the index structure. *ProbeInput* provides the next data to be processed. Depending on the input data characteristics, the build input is instantiated of either type *BTree* if a persistent index exists or else *GJoin-*

3.3 G-Join in Detail

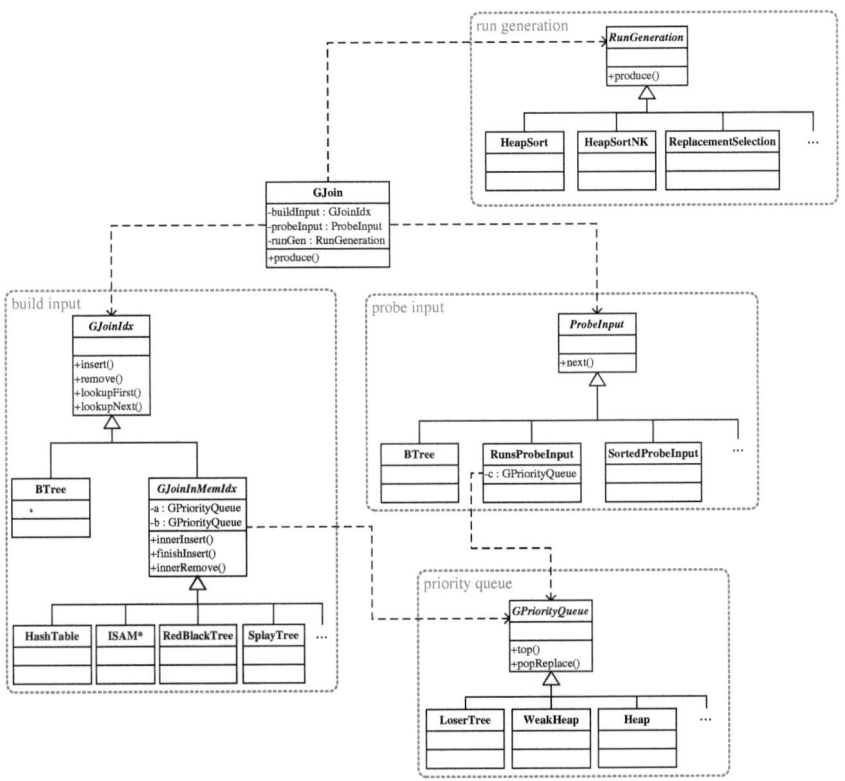

Figure 3.6: Overview of design alternatives for run generation, priority queues, build input, and probe input

InMemIdx if a temporary in-memory index is built. In the latter case, the priority queues A and B also have to be maintained by the index structure. In the current implementation, the in-memory index structure can be of type *HashTable*, *ISAM**[8], *RedBlackTree*, or *SplayTree*. The probe input is instantiated from either type *BTree*, *RunsProbeInput*, or *SortedProbeInput* according to the input characteristics. If runs were generated for the probe input, i.e., in the case of *RunsProbeInput*, priority queue C is needed to guide processing. For generating sorted runs, i.e., **run-generation** in Algorithm 3.3, we implemented *HeapSort*, *HeapSortNK*[9], and *ReplacementSelection*. The priority queues guiding the updates of the main memory index structure and the processing of the probe input are implemented as either *LoserTree*, *WeakHeap*, or *Heap*. Additional instantiations can be added by extending the parent types.

---

[8] *ISAM** is a sort-based index structure similar to Index Sequential Access Method (ISAM).
[9] *HeapSortNK* corresponds to *HeapSort* extended by poor man's normalized keys (see Figure 3.7) for efficient key comparisons.

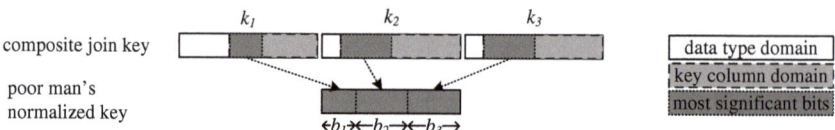

Figure 3.7: Computation of "poor man's normalized key" for a composite join key $\langle k_1, k_2, k_3 \rangle$ where b_i bits are assigned to each join key column k_i

Run Generation Phase

G-join for unsorted (and unindexed) inputs initially generates sorted runs by employing external merge sort and omitting (most of) the merge phase(s). When using a load-sort-store algorithm, the input data is partitioned into chunks small enough to fit in main memory. Each of these chunks is subsequently read into main memory and sorted by an internal sorting algorithm. Obviously, the size of the resulting runs is constrained by the main memory size. An alternative to load-sort-store variants for producing sorted runs is replacement selection. Using this method, the input data is fed through an in-memory priority queue. Each time the top element is extracted, it is replaced by the next input tuple. If the new tuple cannot contribute to the current run, i.e., its key is greater than the last output tuple's key, it is marked as belonging to the next run. As soon as a marked tuple reaches the top of the priority queue, a new run is started. For uniformly distributed key values, replacement selection produces runs of length twice the priority queue (and thus main memory) size. The advantages of replacement selection over load-sort-store algorithms are of particular interest for g-join: First, replacement selection generates sorted runs of length approximately two times memory size whereas load-sort-store algorithms produce runs of length equal to memory size. This implies that only about half as many runs are generated for each input compared to load-sort-store. The memory requirements of g-join during the join phase are proportional to the number of left runs and thus halving the number of runs halves the memory utilized by the operator. Second, when inputs are (partly) presorted, replacement selection generates even longer runs than twice the memory size, in the extreme only a single run. In contrast, load-sort-store variants do not take advantage of this. Knuth (1973) covers replacement selection in detail and illuminates optimization potential. Further, work by Larson and Graefe (1998) and Larson (2003) extended classical replacement selection to work for variable-length tuples and Martinez-Palau et al. (2010) published a replacement selection version creating long runs in a stable way, i.e., independent of the input data characteristics like inversely sorted keys.

The most expensive operation in sorting is the comparison of sort keys, in particular when they consist of multiple (possibly non-integer) values. In such cases, it is advisable to base sorting on a hash code of the join keys. Thereby, however, one is giving up on the fuzzy ordering of the output. Alternatively, the use of "poor man's normalized keys" as introduced by Graefe and Larson (2001) and Lomet (2001) enables more efficient comparisons. Figure 3.7 illustrates how poor man's normalized keys are generated from the given join key values during the run generation phase. For a composite join key $\langle k_1, k_2, k_3 \rangle$, the normalized key is partitioned into bit ranges of sizes b_1, b_2, b_3 where the size b_i of each range is chosen according to the join key column domain. In the example,

3.3 G-Join in Detail

the domain of join key column k_1 is significantly smaller than the other key column domains so that fewer bits are allocated to the first part b_1 of the normalized key. The b_i most significant bits of each key column k_i are included in the normalized key.

We employ *ReplacementSelection* using weak-heaps in the run generation phase. Sorting based on weak-heaps has been shown to be the fastest heapsort variant by Edelkamp and Wegener (2000) among those considered. Furthermore, we make use of poor man's normalized keys for efficient compare operations. We further consider *HeapSort* and heap sort using normalized keys, denoted *HeapSortNK*, as load-sort-store alternatives to replacement selection and evaluate their performance. Heap sort provides an average and worst case complexity of $\mathcal{O}(n \log n)$ and is thus conform with the robustness claims of g-join.

During run generation, we keep track of some additional information: (1) The highest value per page is stored in the page header so that it can quickly be compared to the upper bound of the immediate join key range to determine if the index structure has to be updated. Otherwise, the index structure would be updated as soon as the first probe value exceeding the immediate join key range is found. (2) The lowest value per run is logged for the initialization of priority queue C. Otherwise, an arbitrary minimum value for all runs would have to be used and the result would be less sorted for the first pages.

Keeping track of the data does not incur much overhead (little time to write minimum values per run and little space to store a pointer to the high value per page). Besides, the algorithm does also work without this information.

Join Phase

Probe Index. If no persistent index on the relevant join columns exists, g-join maintains an in-memory index structure for the build input, which it probes with tuples of the probe input. A lookup operation is processed for each single tuple of the (larger) probe input and the probe index is frequently updated to contain the current immediate join key range at any point in time during join processing. This requires an efficient implementation of the operations for looking up, inserting, and deleting a tuple.

Hash tables are a common choice as they provide an average complexity of $\mathcal{O}(1)$ for all operations. In particular with respect to g-join, there are no "hidden costs" for dynamic resizing as the available main memory is known in advance and completely allocated to the index structure, and the size of the immediate join key range can be anticipated well. We choose *HashTable* as default probe index structure and implement the eviction of left input tuples from the hash table in an eager way. Each time a page is unfixed and discarded from the buffer pool, we first iterate through the page and remove the respective entry in the hash table for every tuple. We propose two alternative update methods that obviate the need for iterating through a page in order to remove entries. These methods can also be applied in combination. (1) The "lazy" hash table update defers the work to be done when a left input page in the buffer pool is unfixed to future insert operations. When removing the page, no work at all has to be done. We expect future inserts to create collisions and detect outdated hash table entries during collision handling. In order to recognize an outdated tuple, however, we need to store the join keys in the hash table (as the referenced tuple is no longer buffer-pool-resident and thus cannot be read anymore). (2) The use of multiple hash tables allows for deleting a whole hash table and unfixing buffer pool pages in bulks as soon as its key range moves out of the immediate join key range. Of course, we need to probe into all hash tables. For particular join cases, optimizations are possible. In case there exists a 1:N relationship between the input relations and 1 being the functionality of the smaller input, a zigzag search as described in Helmer et al. (1998) is appropriate.

We further implement and evaluate three alternative ordered indexes which, unlike hash tables, are unsusceptible to duplication skew and thus comply with the robustness claims of g-join. Moreover, they exhibit a certain locality of reference, which is exploited by g-join as tuples are joined (roughly) in ascending join key order. The *ISAM** index is similar to ISAM indexes[10] and maintains a list of chunks $C_1, \ldots, C_n$. The entries within the index are totally ordered by key value. That is, the entries within each chunk C_i are sorted and the key ranges of the chunks are disjoint. Further, it holds that keys within preceding chunks $C_j, j < i$, are smaller than keys in C_i and that keys within following chunks $C_k, k > i$, are larger than keys in C_i. *ISAM** uses binary search to both determine the correct chunk and to find the searched entry within the chunk. It therefore requires logarithmic time with respect to the index size for the lookup operation. Insert operations merge entries on pages to be loaded from different left input runs within a new chunk and append it to the index. As merging requires generating the total order for the new items, the insert operation is in time $\mathcal{O}(n \log n)$ with respect to the new chunk's size n. The delete operations simply prune the low-end chunks of the index and can be done in constant time. Besides the *ISAM** index, we examine a *RedBlackTree* and a *SplayTree* as representatives for tree-based index structures. They provide logarithmic lookup, insert, and delete complexity. In particular, the splay tree property, i.e., recently accessed entries are accessed again more quickly than others, is interesting to g-join.

Priority Queues. G-join for an unindexed build input maintains the priority queues A and B to decide upon loading data into and discarding it from the buffer pool and the in-memory probe index structure. Further, if runs are generated for the probe input, priority queue C guides the processing order of the runs' pages. Priority queues are typically implemented as a heap structure providing an average complexity of $\mathcal{O}(\log n)$, where n is the number of elements in the queue, for inserting an element and extracting the element with the highest priority. By relaxing the requirements for a heap, Dutton (1992) defined a data structure called weak-heap, which reduces the number of comparisons needed. Dutton (1993) applies weak-heaps to sorting and shows that they exhibit the least number of comparisons among the considered algorithms weak-heapsort, bottom-up heapsort, and quicksort. Knuth (1973) presents loser trees, a tournament tree variant, as an alternative for an efficient merge phase in external sort algorithms. Compared to traditional heaps, loser trees require fewer comparisons for re-establishing their heap property, because loser trees implement each update operation with a single leaf-to-root pass. Loser trees have been widely adopted and even implemented into IBM mainframes using vector registers by Garcia et al. (1994).

Despite the optimizations within weak-heaps and loser trees, the priority queue structures we consider all exhibit logarithmic time for updates. We implement *LoserTree*, *WeakHeap*, and *Heap* structures and compare their performance.

Run Sizes and Key Value Distribution Skew. G-join usually requires only little main memory during the join phase. In particular, the build input tuples within the

---

[10]A description of the index-sequential access method (ISAM) can be found in Ramakrishnan and Gehrke (2003).

3.3 G-Join in Detail

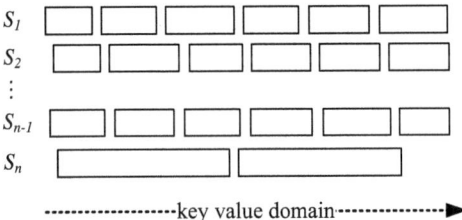

Figure 3.8: Illustration of the "last run problem": the key ranges spanned by pages ☐ of the last run S_n are much larger than the key ranges on pages of the other runs while the number of tuples • per page is the same for all runs

current immediate join key range are main-memory-resident while the join is computed. For sorted probe inputs, either output by a previous sort operator or read from a sorted index, the immediate join key range consists only of one key value at any point in time so that two pages of each build input run suffice to perform the probe. However, when runs are generated from the probe input and these runs are processed page by page, the key value distribution on each of the run pages determines how large the immediate join key range has to be expanded to join one page.

Join key ranges on a single page may vary due to skewed data or different run lengths, e.g., a short last run[11]. Figure 3.8 illustrates this effect for n runs of input S denoted S_1 to S_n. Each page holds three tuples (represented by the bullet points). However, the pages of the last run S_n span a much larger key range than the pages of the other runs. Thus, a page of run S_n requires more pages to be loaded from the left input than a page of runs $S_1, S_2, \ldots, S_{n-1}$. When the next page of S_n is processed, the key range is extended to at least the key range of this page. However, the join key range will shrink again slowly, as pages can only be removed from the in-memory index structure as soon as the next pages of each of the runs S_1 to S_{n-1} have been processed.

There are different approaches to solve this issue. First, additional merge steps after run generation have effects on both inputs. There will be less runs from the left input and thus more than two pages per run will fit into the buffer pool. The runs from the right input will be longer and have a smaller key range per page, thus requiring fewer pages from the left input in the buffer pool during join processing. The second approach to varying key ranges is to handle them during join processing. One possibility is to provide an extra buffer pool frame for pages of the last S run and keep one page of this run loaded permanently. While the immediate join key range moves on guided by the other runs' pages, the entries of the page currently covered by the immediate join key range are processed. A more general solution to skew is to load only an affordable amount of data from the left input into memory and to process as much of the right input as possible. Page processing is preempted if the page key range exceeds the immediate join key range. In this case, priority queue C is updated with the last processed entry as sort key and the currently processed page is unfixed. It will be processed further when its priority queue entry reaches the top position of the queue (again).

---

[11]The last run may be very short but it may nevertheless cover almost the complete key range, i.e., the key ranges on its pages are very large compared to the other runs.

We implemented the preemption of page processing for cases in which the immediate join key range is not large enough to completely join the current right input page. This solution not only prevents the hash table from overload but also enables handling of skewed data in general. As a first straightforward approach, we let the buffer pool grow as required until the number of pages in the buffer pool reaches the threshold of two times the number of left input runs. After that, we load at most one more page from the left input for each currently processed right input page. We then process the tuples on the current page that are in the immediate join key range. When we read a join key that exceeds the immediate join key range, we stop processing the page, update priority queue C with the largest processed join key, and unload the page from the buffer pool. It will be loaded again as soon as the immediate join key range allows further processing.

3.3.3 Outer, Semi, Anti Semi Joins

We integrated a full g-join implementation into HyPer/dbcore including semi joins and anti semi joins as well as left outer, right outer, and full outer joins. The join variants, which are described in more detail in Graefe (2012), require only few extensions like an additional bit in order to keep track of which tuples have already found a join partner. We only sketch the required changes to standard inner join $R \bowtie S$ with R being the build input and S the probe input in the following.

Outer Joins

Outer joins bring together matching tuples like inner joins and, in addition, they produce output tuples for input data that didn't find a join partner. The left (build input) outer join $R \bowtie S$ requires a flag bit in the in-memory index entries indicating whether the entry already took part in the join or not. Each time a regular join output tuple is generated, the index entry flag is set. When the index is updated according to priority queue B, i.e., entries are evicted, this flag is checked and an output tuple is produced if the flag is not set. After all right input tuples have been processed, the index is traversed a last time to find unmatched build input tuples. The right (probe input) outer join $R \bowtie S$ is straightforward as it can be decided at the time a tuple is processed whether it found a join partner or an extra output tuple has to be returned.

Semi Joins

Semi joins produce output for tuples of one of the inputs which find a join partner in the other input. In contrast to inner joins, one input tuple may produce at most one output tuple. For this purpose, the left (build input) semi join $R \bowtie S$ requires a flag bit in the in-memory index entries indicating whether the entry already took part in the join or not. If so, the entry will not produce any output again. If the flag is not set and a probe input tuple matches, an output tuple is produced and the flag is set. For the right (probe input) semi join $R \bowtie S$, the build input is probed until one match is found and an output tuple is generated. As the tuple may not produce any further output, probing for its key is aborted at this point.

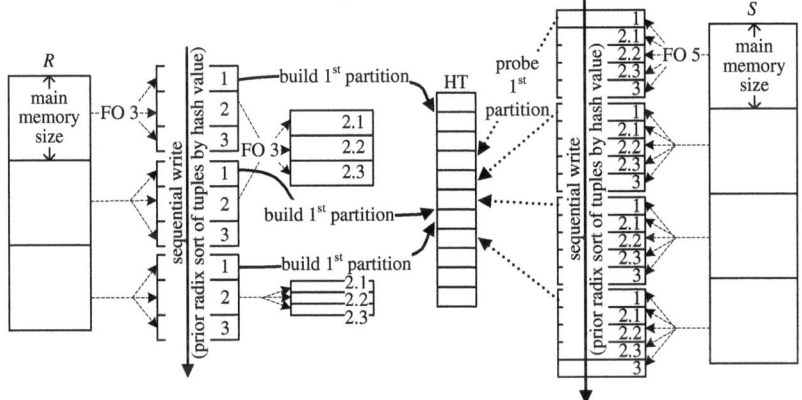

Figure 3.9: Hash join in HyPer/dbcore: left and right input sizes are three and four times main memory size, respectively; the initial as well as the re-partitioning fan-out (FO) is 3

Anti Semi Joins

Anti semi joins are the opposite of semi joins. Output is produced for input tuples that do not find a join partner in the other input. The left (build input) anti semi join $R \triangleright S$ requires a flag bit in the in-memory index entries indicating whether the entry already found a join partner or not. Each time a probe input tuple matches, the flag for the corresponding index entry is set. When the index is updated according to priority queue B, i.e., entries are evicted, this flag is checked and an output tuple is produced if the flag is not set. After all right input tuples have been processed, the index is traversed a last time to find unmatched build input tuples. The right (probe input) anti semi join $R \triangleleft S$ is straightforward as it can be decided at the time a tuple is processed whether it found a join partner or – in case no join partner at all was found – an output tuple has to be returned.

3.4 Traditional Join Algorithms

We briefly present the HyPer/dbcore implementations of hash join, sort-merge join, and index nested-loops join, and summarize the main characteristics of g-join in comparison to the traditional algorithms.

3.4.1 Hash Join

Figure 3.9 illustrates the functioning of the hash join implementation in HyPer/dbcore. It is basically a GRACE hash join as presented in Kitsuregawa et al. (1983) and Fushimi et al. (1986), generating partitions from the build and probe inputs and then joining the corresponding partitions. However, there are some specifics making the hash join implementation more robust and efficient. The build input is loaded into memory until either no more tuples are left or the input exceeds the memory size. If the build input fits into memory, it is converted into a hash table in-place and the probe input is pipelined, probing into the hash table with each tuple. If the build input exceeds memory, the build input tuples are range-partitioned by hash value into a predefined number of partitions, similar to radix sort. In the example in Figure 3.9, a fan-out of 3 is used, denoted by "FO 3". Using this partitioning scheme ensures robustness with respect to (distribution) skew. Further, it enables the sequential write of partition chunks. Thereby, the random and sequential I/O phases of standard hash join are switched as partition chunks are written out sequentially but re-collecting the partition chunks during the join phase results in (partly) random I/O. The rest of the build input is processed in the same way: tuples are loaded into memory until no space is left, the data is sorted and partitioned by hash value, and partition chunks are written to disk sequentially. If the resulting partitions still do not fit into memory (this is the case for partition 2 in Figure 3.9), another partition phase is initiated. Each build input partition is read in chunk after chunk and processed in the same way as during the first partition phase (resulting in the three sub-partitions 2.1 to 2.3 for partition 2). Here again, the partitioning fan-out is predefined and constant. In Figure 3.9, we used "FO 3" as for the initial partitioning. After partitioning of the build input results in partitions small enough to fit into memory, the final partition ranges are used to partition the probe input in one partition phase. We do not consider the case that a build input partition cannot be further partitioned and does not fit into memory as it is the case when the whole partition consists of values with the same key. Probe input tuples are loaded into memory until there is no space left. Then, they are range-partitioned using the known partition ranges. This results in only one partitioning phase for the probe input, no matter how large it is. In Figure 3.9, the probe input is directly split up into five final partitions. Note that these partitions do not have to fit into memory. During the join phase, each build input partition is loaded into the hash table, i.e., all of the partition's chunks are read and each tuple is placed into a hash table bucket according to its hash value. Then, the corresponding partition from the probe input is read and each tuple is used to probe into the hash table for join partners. For the evaluation of hash join, it is important to keep in mind that sequential and random I/O phases are inverted compared to standard hash join implementations as described in Graefe (1993), partitioning occurs on the hash values of the keys, and the right input is not partitioned recursively as the partitioning scheme of the build input is applied in one step.

3.4.2 (Sort-)Merge Join

The sort-merge join implementation in HyPer/dbcore is sketched in Figure 3.10. Sorted runs are generated from the left and right input using replacement selection. Then, the merge phase and the join phase are executed in an integrated manner if memory suffices, i.e., if one page of each run can be kept in memory. If not, some of the runs are combined in an intermediate merge phase. The merge fan-in (FI) is determined by the available memory and the number of runs to be merged. If the number of runs to be merged exceeds the maximum possible fan-in, multiple merge steps are conducted. In the illustration in Figure 3.10, three runs have been generated from the left input and five from the right input. Two of the five right input runs are merged in one step ("FI 2"), so that, in the final integrated merge-and-join phase, three left and four right runs are piped through the respective heaps (labeled "FI 3" and "FI 4"), and their merged outputs are joined. If run generation results in one run for both the left and the right input, we simply iterate through the runs during the join phase and output matching tuples.

3.4 Traditional Join Algorithms

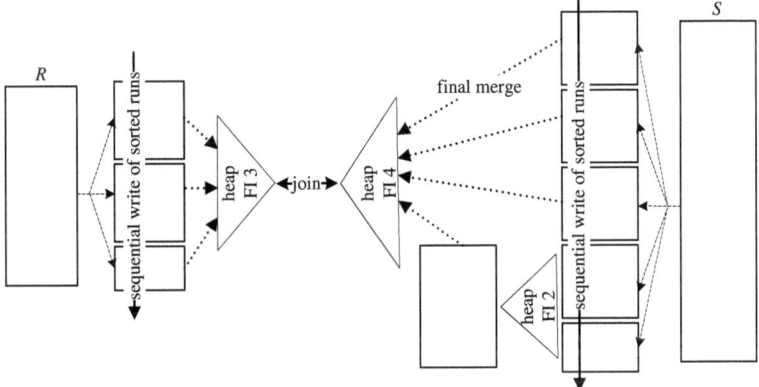

Figure 3.10: Sort-merge join in HyPer/dbcore: run generation results in three runs for the left and five runs for the right input; the intermediate merge fan-in (FI) is 2 and the final merge fan-in is 3 for the left input and 4 for the right input

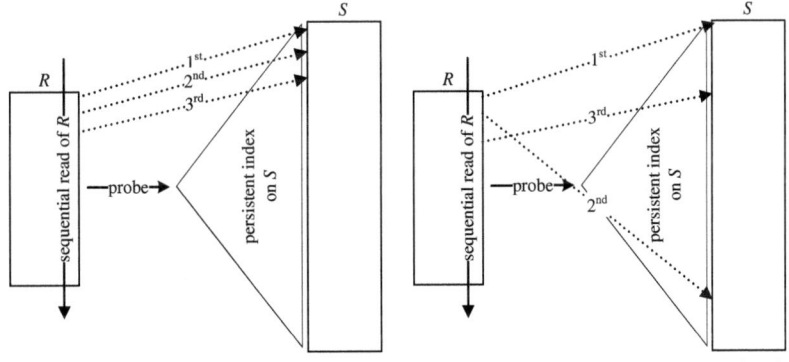

(a) Index nested-loops join with sorted probe input
(b) Index nested-loops join with unsorted probe input

Figure 3.11: Index nested-loops join in HyPer/dbcore: depending on whether the probe input is sorted or not, index accesses are supposed to be served from cache or to cause costly page faults

3.4.3 Index Nested-Loops Join

Figure 3.11 illustrates the index nested-loops join implementation in HyPer/dbcore. For each tuple in the outer input, index nested-loops join probes into the existing index and produces result tuples if matches are found. The index is a B^+-tree containing all

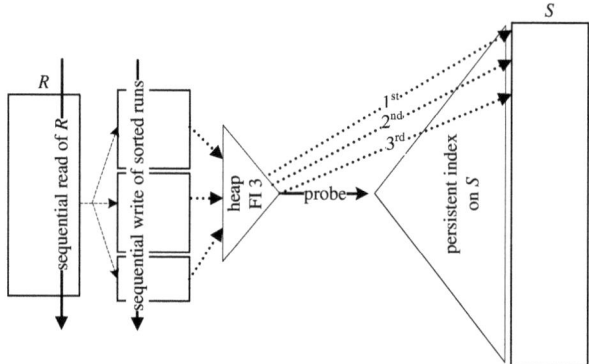

Figure 3.12: Sort-index nested-loops join in HyPer/dbcore: the unsorted probe input is first sorted in order to avoid costly page faults caused by random index accesses

relevant data, not only pointers (TIDs) to the data. The performance of index nested-loops join heavily depends on the amount of cache locality that can be exploited. As sketched in Figure 3.11a, if the outer input is sorted there is a high probability that index pages containing the searched keys are in the cache as neighboring keys have already been searched. In particular, each index leaf page is read once during index nested-loops join processing. If the outer input is unsorted as shown in Figure 3.11b, the index is probed randomly and therefore there is no cache locality. Further, the index leaf pages are likely to be read from disk several times, thereby incurring I/O overhead and affecting the performance negatively. Depending on the size of the outer input, it may thus be advisable to sort it before probing the index as described by DeWitt et al. (1993). The sort-index nested-loops join algorithm is sketched in Figure 3.12. For sorting the outer input, we employ run generation using replacement selection and then merge the runs. The output of the merge phase is directly used as input to index nested-loops join, i.e., no intermediate result is written to disk. However, the merge phase itself may require writing intermediate results to disk. This is the case if the number of runs exceeds the maximum number of runs that can be merged in one pass, i.e., the number of main memory pages available minus one page required for the output.

3.4.4 Summary and Comparison

We summarize the characteristics of g-join, hash join, and sort-merge join discussed in the previous sections in Table 3.3. An extensive discussion of the duality between (traditional) hash join and sort-merge join can be found in Graefe (1993). For index nested-loops join, only the probe input properties are of relevance: The probe input cardinality determines the number of index accesses but only little memory is required during join processing for holding the currently processed tuples. Duplication and distribution skew have practically no impact on the performance, however, as sketched in Figure 3.11, the probe input sort order might highly influence the overall join performance. Further, the output sort order depends on the input sort order.

3.4 Traditional Join Algorithms

Property	Hash join	Sort-merge join	G-join
Input sizes	Left input only determines the recursive partitioning depth	Each input determines its number of merge levels needed	Smaller input only determines the buffer pool requirements (and the potentially required merge steps)
Input sort order	Cannot be exploited	Is exploited	Is exploited
Duplication skew	Impact on recursion depth and partition file sizes and thus memory utilization during join phase if left input contains many duplicate key values	Practically no impact	Impact on buffer pool size and hash table fill factor if smaller input contains many duplicate key values
Distribution skew	Practically no impact in HyPer/dbcore as partitioning employs hash values and is adaptive w.r.t. their ranges	Practically no impact	Impact on buffer pool size and hash table fill factor if key values of the smaller input are very dense
Buffer pool size	Uses all available memory during the partitioning phase and the join phase	Uses all available memory during run generation; during the integrated merge-and-join phase, memory requirements depend on the number of runs	Uses all available memory during run generation; during the join phase, on average only two pages per smaller input run need to be memory-resident at any time
Output	Unsorted	Sorted	Nearly sorted

Table 3.3: Characteristics of hash join, sort-merge join, and g-join in HyPer/dbcore

If the optimizer choices are based on reliable statistics about input sizes and data skew, it will favor hash join in case one of the inputs is small and the other is large. As only the left input size affects the partitioning depth and thus performance, hash join outperforms sort-merge join. Our HyPer/dbcore implementation of hash join even increases the gains as the right input is never partitioned recursively. However, hash join fails to exploit (roughly) sorted inputs as does sort-merge join. Thus, if the data is already sorted or if the output must be sorted on a join key and sorting the result is more expensive than sorting the inputs, sort-merge join will be the optimizer's choice. If there are persistent indexes that can be exploited during join processing, the optimizer chooses index nested-loops join in general.

G-join benefits from sorted inputs or persistent indexes, i.e., qualitative information, and produces nearly sorted output. It exploits different input sizes in terms of memory footprint and processing time. However, knowledge of input sizes, i.e., quantitative information, is not required in advance but gained during run generation and applied for efficient role reversal. The I/O volume of g-join is equal to the I/O volume of hash join.

3.5 Evaluation

We have integrated g-join into the HyPer/dbcore database system and compare its performance to that of the existing traditional join implementations. Our experiments are designed to verify the claims in Graefe (2012). We present the results of in-memory join computation and thoroughly investigate the execution time, memory consumption, and robustness of the join algorithms in a disk-based scenario. We assume that qualitative information is correct and reliable during query optimization, e.g., whether or not a table is indexed and whether an intermediate query result is sorted, but that quantitative information is often unreliable and even misleading, e.g., sizes of intermediate results and thus of join inputs. The inputs in our benchmarks are unsorted if not stated otherwise.

3.5.1 Settings

The benchmarks are run on a commodity server with the following specifications: Dual Intel X5570 Quad-Core-CPU, 8 MB Cache, 64 GB RAM, 16 300 GB SAS-HD, Linux operating system RHEL 5.4. To amplify the interesting effects with data volumes practical in our experimental environment, we restrict the physical RAM to 4 GB by allocating 60 GB of physical RAM to another process, which `mlocks` its assigned memory and thereby makes sure that it is not swapped during the benchmarks.

For the evaluation of the join algorithms, we execute a primary key – foreign key join of the TPC-C benchmark tables `Order` and `OrderLine` (see Figure 3.13) that corresponds to the SQL query

```
SELECT *
FROM Order, OrderLine
WHERE O_W_ID=OL_W_ID
  AND O_D_ID=OL_D_ID
  AND O_ID=OL_O_ID
```

Each of the join algorithms is executed stand-alone. The `Order` and `OrderLine` data is generated such that the column types and the values of the join key columns correspond to the specification. Join attributes are equally distributed. Tuples have a fixed length of 36 bytes for an `Order` tuple, and 65 bytes for an `OrderLine` tuple (due to byte alignment for 64-bit systems, an `Order` tuple allocates 40 bytes and an `OrderLine` tuple allocates 72 bytes on disk). For each `Order` tuple, on average ten matching `OrderLine` tuples are created. In total, there are ten times as many `OrderLine` tuples as `Order` tuples. Those

3.5 Evaluation

column	data type
O_ID	uint32_t
O_D_ID	uint32_t
O_W_ID	uint32_t
O_C_ID	uint32_t
O_ENTRY_ID	uint64_t
O_CARRIER_ID	uint32_t
O_OL_CNT	uint32_t
O_ALL_LOCAL	uint32_t

(a) Order

column	data type
OL_O_ID	uint32_t
OL_D_ID	uint32_t
OL_W_ID	uint32_t
OL_NUMBER	uint32_t
OL_I_ID	uint32_t
OL_SUPPLY_W_ID	uint32_t
OL_DELIVERY_D	uint64_t
OL_QUANTITY	char
OL_AMOUNT	double
OL_DIST_INFO	char[24]

(b) OrderLine

Figure 3.13: Extract of the TPC-C schema

tuples are generated in a random order and thus are not clustered by key value. The input tuples are fed into the join operator without being written to disk first.

We carried out the experiments providing the operator with 10 MB of memory, which are not exceeded during the execution. For the data, we chose the scale factors 250, 500, 750, and 1000 warehouses resulting in the relation cardinalities and the data sizes given in Table 3.4 (these sizes include metadata like run or chunk headers and tuple length). We conduct each experiment five times and report the average execution time of the five repetitions and the average absolute deviation of the single execution times from this value.

scale	Order		OrderLine	
	cardinality	size [MB]	cardinality	size [MB]
250	$7.5 \cdot 10^6$	316	$75 \cdot 10^6$	5453
500	$15 \cdot 10^6$	632	$150 \cdot 10^6$	10906
750	$22.5 \cdot 10^6$	948	$225 \cdot 10^6$	16359
1000	$30 \cdot 10^6$	1264	$300 \cdot 10^6$	21812

Table 3.4: Data scales and sizes for the experiments

3.5.2 G-Join vs. Traditional Join Algorithms

We first investigate the performance of g-join compared to the traditional join algorithms. In this context, we consider well and poorly optimized cases. We further examine the cases in which one of the inputs fits in memory or exceeds memory only slightly. Last, we study the performance of the algorithms when persistent indexes can be exploited.

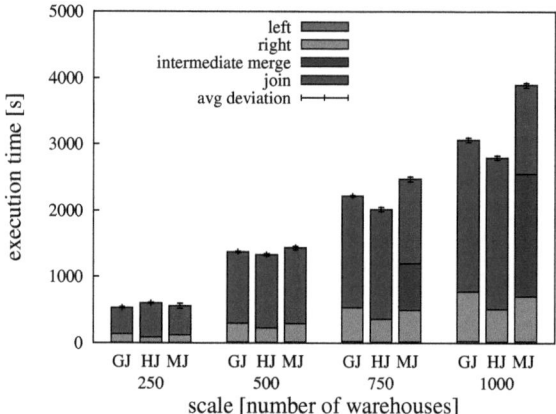

Figure 3.14: Execution time comparison of g-join (GJ), hash join (HJ), and sort-merge join (MJ) on unsorted inputs: g-join and hash join show a comparable performance, the performance of sort-merge join decreases rapidly for larger data scales as intermediate merge steps incur additional I/O

Performance in "Well-Optimized" Cases

We investigate the most interesting question first: Do we lose performance when choosing g-join instead of a traditional algorithm when the traditional algorithm would have been appropriate? The results are illustrated in Figures 3.14 and 3.15.

Unsorted inputs (Figure 3.14): Hash join is the algorithm of choice for unsorted inputs, especially in case of very different data sizes. We therefore compare the join performance when both inputs are unsorted. Order is the smaller of the two relations and thus represents the left input. We configured the partitioning fan-out of hash join so that no recursive partitioning is needed for any data size scale. Sort-merge join employs the largest possible merge fan-in for the integrated merge-and-join as well as intermediate merge steps. For the scales 250 and 500, no intermediate merge steps are required, for scale 750, one and for scale 1000, two intermediate merge steps are conducted.

In total, g-join performs slightly worse than hash join, but the execution times do not differ by more than 9%. Depending on the hash join configuration (e.g., the fan-out, which we manually set but which is usually chosen by the optimizer based on possibly wrong statistics), hash join might have an even longer execution time than g-join. Sort-merge join is competitive to g-join and hash join if no intermediate merge steps (including expensive I/O) are required.

Roughly sorted inputs (Figure 3.15): When inputs are completely sorted, g-join effectively becomes merge join. The more interesting case occurs when inputs are roughly sorted, e.g., when the output of one g-join is the input of another join. In this case, run generation produces one run for the left and one run for the right input. As can be seen in Figure 3.15, the total execution times of g-join are on average 15% longer than those of sort-merge join. This is due to the overhead incurred by hash table updates during the join phase. However, g-join can easily be adapted to omit maintaining the in-memory

3.5 Evaluation

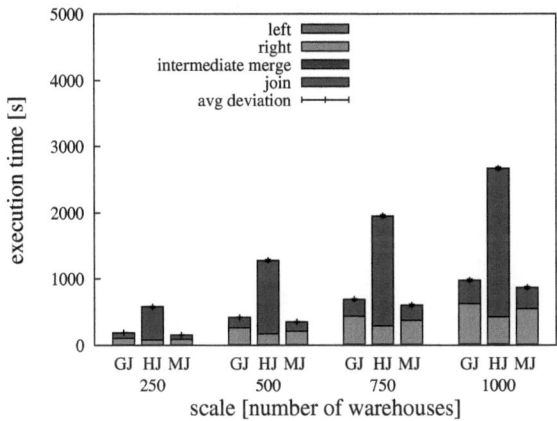

Figure 3.15: Execution time comparison of g-join (GJ), hash join (HJ), and sort-merge join (MJ) on roughly sorted inputs: g-join and sort-merge join take advantage of the (partial) sorting, whereas it has no effect on hash join

index and switch to merge join-like execution in this case. As expected, hash join does not take advantage of sorted inputs and thus is not competitive to g-join and sort-merge join in this case.

Performance in "Poorly Optimized" Cases

The performance of the traditional join algorithms might degrade when the estimates employed by the query optimizer during plan generation are wrong. Two common scenarios for hash join are an unfavorably chosen partitioning fan-out and wrongly estimated input sizes.

If the (initial) partitioning fan-out is chosen too small, re-partitioning is required, which leads to additional reads and writes of the inputs. This additional I/O has a significant impact on performance. If the partitioning fan-out is chosen too large, too many small partitions consisting of too many small (sequential) parts are created. They result in more overhead for building the hash table and don't make efficient use of the memory assigned to the operator. Traditional (GRACE) hash join implementations are susceptive to these kinds of estimation errors. The HyPer/dbcore implementation of hash join, however, does not suffer from this estimation error. It assumes the optimizer to be good at estimating the size ratio of left and right input. By completely partitioning the left (smaller) input before the right input is processed, it avoids re-partitioning the right input because the number of final partitions is known before partitioning starts. The overhead incurred by wrong fan-out estimations is therefore quite small (as long as the smaller input was correctly chosen as the build input) because it only affects the (smaller) left input. Moreover, the join phase benefits from re-partitioning by more sequential and less random I/O.

However, if the optimizer fails in correctly determining build and probe inputs, i.e., the relative input sizes are not estimated correctly, the larger input is recursively partitioned

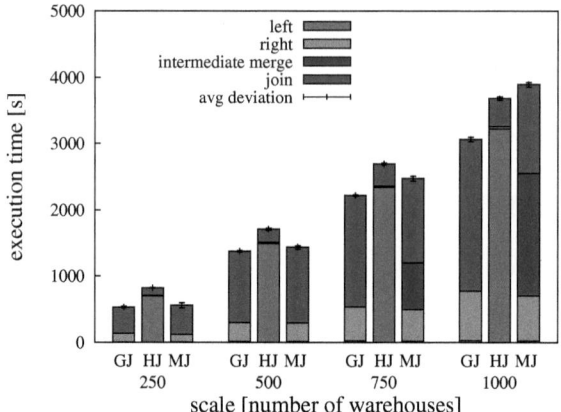

Figure 3.16: Execution time comparison of g-join (GJ), hash join (HJ), and sort-merge join (MJ) when the optimizer wrongly assumes OrderLine to be the smaller relation and assigns it the build role in hash join; g-join and sort-merge join do not suffer from this optimizer mistake due to role reversal

as shown in our experiments in Figure 3.16. The optimistic assumption of correct size ratio estimation impedes efficient role reversal in case of optimizer mistakes, i.e., role reversal before most of the work has been done. Efficient role reversal requires knowing the left and right input sizes before completely processing one of the inputs, which can be provided only when interleaving left and right (possibly recursive) partitioning steps.

Sort-merge join always generates runs for both inputs, merges some of the runs if necessary and finally conducts an integrated merge-and-join phase. Thus, there is no unfavorable case. G-join as well has no "bad" case. If relative input sizes were mistaken, role reversal is possible after run generation. Therefore, the performance numbers for g-join and sort-merge join in Figure 3.16 are the same as in Figure 3.14. The comparison reveals that hash join takes up to 54% longer than g-join (scale 250) if query optimization is poor. Sort-merge join takes up to 27% longer than g-join if inputs are large (scale 1000).

From the results, we conclude that for large unsorted inputs, g-join is more robust than both hash join and sort-merge join: hash join suffers from mistaken optimizer choices (switched build and probe inputs), while the buffer pool requirements of sort-merge join exceed the available memory so that intermediate merge steps have to be conducted. If inputs are roughly sorted, g-join shares the advantages of sort-merge join whereas hash join cannot profit.

In-memory Execution

Join algorithms are executed "in-memory" when no (intermediate) data is written to disk during the join. So far, we considered the cases when g-join, hash join, and sort-merge join are not executed in-memory, but generate intermediate data like sorted runs or partitions on disk. In the case of g-join and hash join, when the smaller of the two inputs fits in main memory, this is not necessary and execution is considerably sped up. An index

3.5 Evaluation

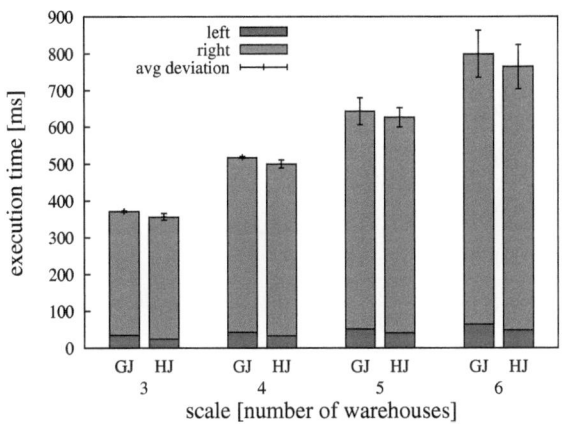

Figure 3.17: G-join and hash join execution times in-memory

structure is built out of the smaller input, the larger input is scanned once and the index structure is probed for every tuple of the larger input to find join partners. No runs are generated in the case of g-join and no partitions in the case of hash join. In our g-join implementation, we use a hash table as probe index structure so that hash join and g-join are quite similar for the in-memory case. For sort-merge join, we do not consider in-memory execution because it would require not only one (the smaller) input to fit in memory but both inputs at once. When joining the relations Order and OrderLine, this means that sort-merge join requires 20 times more data than g-join and hash join to fit in memory in order to execute the computation without intermediate disk writes.

We present the results for the in-memory join in Figure 3.17 up to scale 6, which is the largest scale for which the Order data fits in memory. G-join and hash join show practically equal performance. The slight difference is due to more branches in our g-join implementation.

Hybrid G-join

When data size slightly exceeds the in-memory limit, there is an immense performance decrease as shown in Figure 3.18 (left- and right-most bars). A growth of the Order relation by only 17% (from 6 to 7 warehouses) causes the execution time to increase by a factor of 5 (from ca. 700 ms to ca. 3300 ms). Using hybrid g-join as sketched in Section 3.3.1 with 90% of memory allocated to the maximum heap and 10% to the minimum heap, we can smooth the execution time degradation significantly. Figure 3.18 (middle bar) reports the execution time of hybrid g-join (ca. 1300 ms) in comparison to non-hybrid g-join (ca. 3300 ms) when the left input size slightly exceeds memory (7 warehouses).

As HyPer/dbcore does not include a hybrid hash join implementation, we do not provide a performance comparison of hybrid g-join and hybrid hash join. However, we are confident that the performance evaluation presented proves the effectiveness of our hybrid g-join implementation and the performance impact is comparable to that of the standard hybrid hash join.

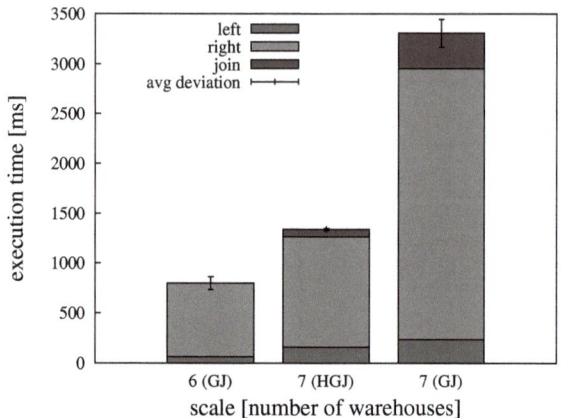

Figure 3.18: Hybrid g-join (HGJ) smooths the execution time increase of g-join (GJ) when the data size slightly exceeds the memory size

Using Persistent Indexes

If the tables to be joined have indexes on the join key, index nested-loops join is one of the choices of the optimizer. We conducted experiments exploiting an existing index on all relevant columns of the right `OrderLine` input. The results are shown in Figure 3.19. We chose to present the execution times using the same scale on the y-axis as in the other experiments for ease of comparison. For an unsorted non-indexed probe input, g-join takes advantage of the rough sorting achieved by run generation. Probing the index completely randomly – as index nested-loops join – has a huge negative impact on the execution time, which is caused by cache thrashing (see also DeWitt et al. (1993)). We aborted the experiments after two hours. However, when sorting the probe input before starting the join phase, index nested-loops join shows a much better performance, in particular as the probe input is comparatively small and sorting does not incur much overhead. In total, g-join performs much better than naïve index nested-loops join and is comparable to a specialized sort-index nested-loops join. Obviously, hash join would not gain any benefits. Sort-merge join behaves as sort-index nested-loops join. Thus, g-join again exhibits its stable behavior of being close to the best specialized solution.

We conclude that g-join takes advantage of existing indexes like index nested-loops join, but in addition benefits from run generation. Probing the index in a (roughly) sorted way guarantees high cache locality during the join phase.

3.5.3 Design Alternatives

In Section 3.3.2, we discussed several design alternatives regarding run generation, probe index, and priority queues. We now examine the impact of the alternative implementations on the performance of g-join. The default configuration is to use replacement selection with normalized keys for run generation, a hash table as probe index, and loser trees as priority queues. We differ from this default only in one dimension in each experiment.

3.5 Evaluation

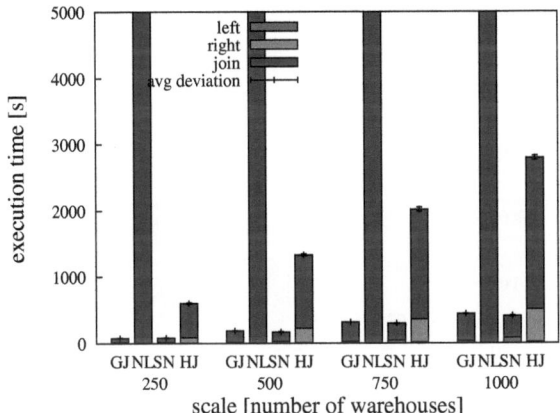

Figure 3.19: Execution time comparison of g-join (GJ), index nested-loops join (NL), sort-index nested-loops join (SN), which sorts the probe input before joining, and hash join (HJ): for unsorted probe input, GJ takes advantage of the rough sort order achieved by run generation; SN achieves even better performance by completely sorting the probe input; HJ does not benefit from the index

Run Generation

We analyze the run generation phase using heap sort (HS), heap sort with poor man's normalized keys (HK), and replacement selection (RS) with poor man's normalized keys. In Figure 3.20, we compare the execution times of g-join for the different run generation implementations. We find that the performance difference is measurable but not practically significant.

In order to gain a better insight, we list relevant statistical numbers collected during the execution in Table 3.5. For HS, 39% of the CPU time is spent on the comparison of keys. For HK and RS, the comparisons only account for 0.1%, respectively 0.2% of the CPU time.[12] Although the reduction of CPU time is remarkable, the effect on the overall execution time is not significant. This is due to g-join being I/O-bound in this experiment and making use of asynchronous I/O (write back) during run generation. However, in multi-user scenarios, the free processing resources can effectively be exploited by parallel processes. During run generation, the use of normalized keys reduces the number of full key comparisons as shown in Table 3.5. Most of the heapify operations can be conducted on behalf of normalized keys (NK) comparisons. To compare a composite key consisting of three unsigned values, at most six unsigned comparisons are required. However, we observed that on average only 2.7 comparisons were conducted using HS so that the gain using normalized keys (conducting only one comparison) is moderate. For HK and RS, a full comparison is only done when the normalized keys comparison does not suffice, i.e., when the keys are equal in our experiment.

---

[12] These values have been determined using `gprof`.

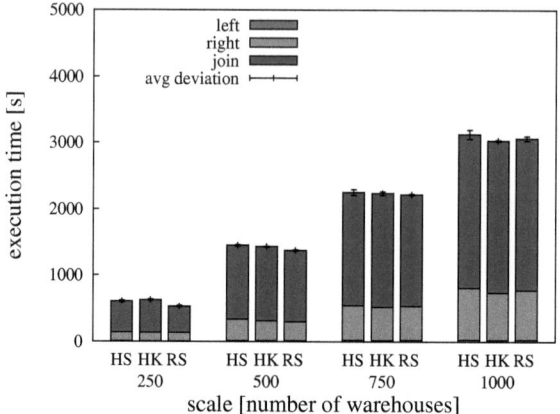

Figure 3.20: Execution time comparison of g-join using heap sort (HS), heap sort with poor man's normalized keys (HK), and replacement selection (RS) during run generation: the use of normalized keys and replacement selection shows only slight positive effects on the execution times despite large CPU savings; this is due to g-join being I/O-bound and because of asynchronous write-back

	HS	HK	RS
# key comparisons (run generation)	4 110 690 239	969 753	1 883 273
# NK comparisons (run generation)	0	4 094 114 682	4 582 574 509
avg # unsigned comparisons per key comparison (run generation)	2.7	6.0	6.0
gprof: % of CPU time attributed to comparisons (run generation)	39	0.1	0.2
# R runs	103	112	57
# S runs	1 717	1 803	902
# key comparisons (priority queues)	12 643 693	12 711 098	11 373 366

Table 3.5: Analysis of run generation alternatives heap sort (HS), heap sort with poor man's normalized keys (HK), and replacement selection (RS) with respect to key comparisons (scale 750)

During the join phase, the number of build and probe input runs is crucial for the memory requirements of g-join. The less runs have to be managed, the less data needs to be maintained in the in-memory index at any time to enable join processing. Furthermore, as a side effect, the number of runs determines the number of entries in the priority queues. The smaller the priority queues, the less key comparisons are required for priority queue updates which has a (slight) positive effect on execution time. In our experiment, HK

3.5 Evaluation

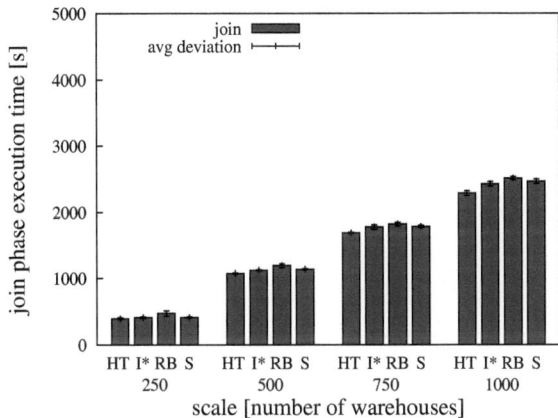

Figure 3.21: Join phase execution time comparison of g-join using a hash table (HT), the ISAM* data structure (I*), a red-black tree (RB), and a splay tree (S) as in-memory index structure during the join phase: for uniformly distributed data, the performance using the different index structures does not differ significantly

results in a few more runs than HS because the tuples including the meta-data (i.e., the normalized key) are larger and thus less tuples fit in the in-memory heap structure for run generation. RS results in approximately half as many runs for both inputs. We further measured the savings in priority queue key comparisons to be approximately 10% when employing replacement selection. The join phase relevant numbers are listed in the second part of Table 3.5.

We conclude that, due to g-join being I/O-bound in this experiment, the gains in terms of execution time that can be achieved by implementing run generation efficiently are of no practical significance. However, in more CPU-bound or multi-user scenarios, we expect g-join and parallel processes to profit from employing replacement selection using normalized keys. Further, when considering non-integer keys, comparisons on integer normalized keys are advisable. In terms of memory consumption, the use of replacement selection pays off in our experiment. The number of (left) input runs and thus the main memory required during the join phase halves compared to heap sort run generation.

Probe Index

We implemented a hash table (HT) and three sort-based index structures as in-memory probe index alternatives: ISAM* (I*), red-black tree (RB), and splay tree (S). We first analyze the performance of g-join using the different index structures on uniformly distributed input data. The results are given in Figure 3.21. In order to abstract from execution time deviations in the run generation phases, we report only the join phase execution time. We find that the execution times do not differ significantly. This again is mainly due to the I/O-bound execution scenario in our experiment. Depending on the

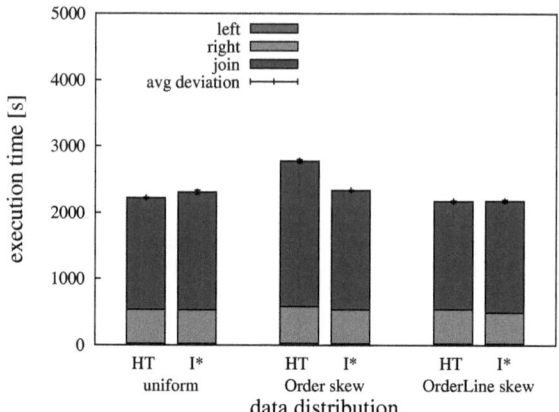

Figure 3.22: Execution time comparison of g-join on uniform data, on skewed Order data, and on skewed OrderLine data (scale 750): when using a hash table (HT), skewed Order data causes large collision chains and thus decreased performance; with an ISAM* (I*) index, the performance does not suffer; skewed OrderLine data has no effect on the performance

hash function, hash tables may be superior to sort-based index structures in terms of CPU time as they perform less key comparisons.

However, hash tables are sensitive to skew, in particular duplication skew. Figure 3.22 compares the execution times of g-join on uniform data (left), on skewed Order data (middle), and on skewed OrderLine data (right) for the scale 750. Skew has been introduced to both Order and OrderLine data using a Zipf distribution with $z = 1.15$ on the three key columns, i.e., 78% of the OrderLine tuples have keys within the lower 12% of the key domain. Introducing skew in the Order data left some dangling references in the OrderLine table. When running the experiments with skewed Order data, we had to increase the memory assigned to the in-memory join index. Doubling it was sufficient for executing the join for the scales 250, 500, 750, and 1000. The total memory consumption still didn't exceed the memory assigned to the operator. As expected, skewed OrderLine data (right input) does not affect the performance. Skewed Order data shows to be very disadvantageous in the join phase if a hash table is employed as in-memory index. This is due to large collision chains. The sort-based ISAM* in-memory index does not suffer from skewed input data.

Priority Queues

During the join phase, g-join employs priority queues to guide the updates of the in-memory index structure and the processing of right input pages. We compare the effect of the priority queue alternatives loser tree (LT), heap (H), and weak-heap (WH) on the performance of g-join in Figure 3.23 and Table 3.6. In order to abstract from execution time deviations in the run generation phases, we report only the join phase execution time.

3.5 Evaluation

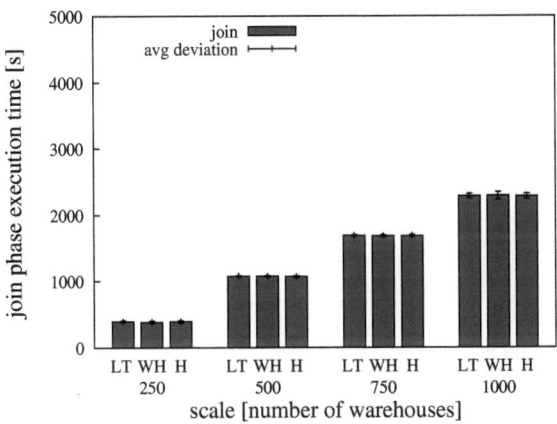

Figure 3.23: Join phase execution time comparison of g-join using loser trees (LT), weak-heaps (WH), and heaps (H) as priority queues during the join phase: due to g-join being I/O-bound the effect on execution time is negligible

	LT	H	WH
# key comparisons (priority queues)	11 373 366	20 119 483	11 372 562

Table 3.6: Analysis of priority queue alternatives loser trees (LT), heaps (H), and weak-heaps (WH) with respect to key comparisons (scale 750)

Again, the execution times do not differ significantly. However, the number of priority queue key comparisons using loser trees or weak-heaps almost halves compared to the use of heaps. We conclude from our experiments that using loser trees or weak-heaps is advantageous in terms of CPU time.

Conclusions

From the experiments in this section, we conclude that the effect of design alternatives regarding run generation, in-memory probe index, and priority queues on the execution time of g-join is negligible in I/O-bound scenarios. However, as main memory capacities are growing fast and thus data access latency is decreasing, the alternatives will be interesting for future architectures. In particular, we found the following: (1) The use of poor man's normalized keys reduces the CPU time of the run generation phase remarkably. Further, replacement selection produces only half as many runs compared to heap sort, which halves the memory requirements of g-join during the join phase. (2) Sort-based in-memory probe indexes perform comparable to hash tables when input data is uniformly distributed. In the presence of duplication skew, however, hash tables suffer from large collision chains. By contrast, sort-based structures are not sensitive to skew. (3) Loser trees and weak-heaps require only half as many key comparisons as heaps and are thus preferable in CPU-bound scenarios.

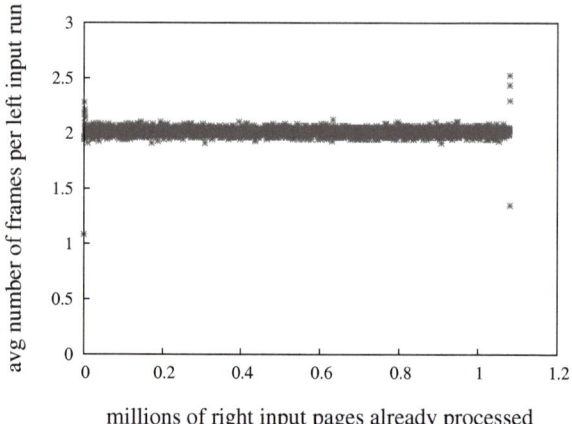

Figure 3.24: Average number of buffer pool frames per left input run during the join phase of g-join (scale 750)

3.5.4 Memory Requirements

In this section, we analyze the memory requirements of g-join compared to the traditional join algorithms. Further, we examine the effectiveness of page processing preemption in limiting the memory requirements of g-join in the presence of skew, in particular with respect to the last-run problem.

Memory Consumption

Our investigation of the memory consumption of g-join, hash join, and sort-merge join considers the situation that the operator is assigned memory of size M. Hash join typically uses all available memory during the whole execution time. During partitioning the left and right input, data is loaded into the available memory and partitioning only starts if an overflow occurs. The partitioning fan-out is chosen such that each created (left) partition has a size approximately equal to the available memory and thus exploits it at its best.

Sort-merge join employs all available memory during run generation. If only one run is generated for the left and for the right input, only one page per input is required during the join phase as the sorted runs are scanned sequentially to find matching tuples. If intermediate merge steps are needed, the required memory depends on how many runs need to be merged. The same applies to the final integrated merge-and-join phase.

G-join also uses all memory during run generation. During the join phase, we expect on average only two pages per left input run to be resident in memory. Remember that the currently processed page from the right input triggers the update of the in-memory index structure as required by the join key range on the page. There are several ways to adjust memory consumption during the join phase. As described in Section 3.3.2, merge steps after run generation reduce the number of runs and thus the average buffer pool requirements. Alternatively, we can provide a dedicated buffer pool frame for pages of

3.5 Evaluation

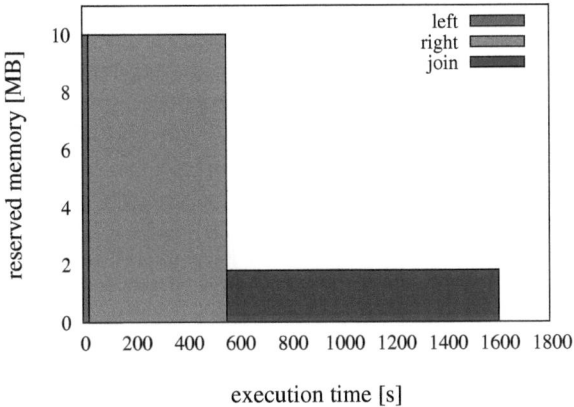

Figure 3.25: G-join memory footprint (scale 750)

scale	memory footprint [MB-seconds]		
	g-join	hash join	sort-merge join
250	2 110	6 120	3 685
500	2 406	13 500	13 970
750	3 764	20 630	20 880
1000	15 102	30 210	42 190

Table 3.7: MB-seconds of g-join, hash join, and sort-merge join for unsorted inputs with different scales

the last right input run. Further, page processing may be preempted if the required key range would incur a heavy increase in the number of buffer-pool-resident pages from the left input. In this case, the page will be re-read and processing will be resumed later, i.e., we trade the buffer pool size for execution preemption and resumption.

We implemented page processing preemption as a universal solution to both buffer pool size limitation and skew handling. The reported experiments were conducted using page processing preemption as follows: Right input pages trigger growth of the buffer pool until it contains twice as many pages as there are left input runs. Then, only at most one additional left input page is loaded into the buffer pool per **process-page** call. This avoids fast increase of the buffer pool size for right input pages with exceptionally large key ranges like the pages of the last run (see Section 3.3.2), but it does not generally limit the buffer pool size. Figure 3.24 shows that the average number of buffer-pool-resident pages per left input run during the join phase is about 2.

In analogy to energy consumption measurement in kWh, we introduce a new measurement unit to rate the memory consumption of the different join algorithms called MB-seconds. Figure 3.25 illustrates it based on the experiments presented in Section 3.5.2 running g-join with 10 MB of memory and a scale of 750 warehouses. During run generation, g-join uses the whole available memory, i.e., 10 MB. The join phase however, requires only 1.8 MB (two frames per left input run). We denote the integral of the memory footprint over time as the MB-seconds. The MB-seconds of g-join, hash join, and sort-merge join are compared in Table 3.7 based on the execution times given in Figure 3.14. The algorithms reserve all memory during the first phase (run generation or partitioning), but g-join requires the least memory during the join phase and therefore has the smallest memory footprint over time.

The Last-Run Problem

We examine the effectiveness of page processing preemption with respect to the "last-run problem" described in Section 3.3.2. Table 3.8 gives an overview of the run lengths and the minimum and maximum join key values per right input run for the data scale 750.[13] The domains of the join key columns are $[1, scale]$ for O_W_ID, $[1, 10]$ for O_D_ID, and $[1, 3\,000]$ for O_ID.

run id	load ops per page	length [pages]	min key	max key
0	9.31	999	[1, 1, 72]	[750, 10, 2 972]
1	0.16	1 133	[1, 1, 515]	[750, 10, 2 899]
2-899	⌀0.02	⌀1 162	[1, 1, 1]	[750, 10, 3 000]
900	0.01	1 153	[1, 1, 120]	[750, 10, 2 770]
901	50.86	450	[1, 1, 82]	[659, 4, 1 269]

Table 3.8: Statistics about right input runs (scale 750)

Pages of the first and in particular the last run let the buffer pool increase extremely because of their larger key value ranges and thus, the larger immediate join key range they require. As given in Table 3.8, for each page of the first run, on average 9.31 left input pages are loaded and for each page of the last run, even 50.86 left input pages are loaded. This extreme increase (compared to the average increase of less than one induced by pages of the other runs) is problematic because the buffer pool shrinks again only slowly after the pages with smaller keys from all runs have been processed. Figure 3.26 illustrates the buffer pool growth in case no limit is enforced on its size. The join execution is aborted due to hash table overflow. If page processing preemption is enabled, the buffer pool size is as shown in Figure 3.24. Skipping the first and last right input run in the join computation has the same effect on the buffer pool as shown in Figure 3.27, i.e., the average number of buffer-pool-resident left input pages is about 2 at any time during the join phase. The results show the effect of different run lengths on the buffer pool size and prove page processing preemption to be effective in handling key value skew.

---

[13]Replacement selection is known to produce runs of almost equal length except for the first and the last runs. In steady state, replacement selection generates runs of length approximately twice the memory size. Before a steady state is reached (initial ca. 2 runs) and when it gives out (after end of input, last ca. 2 runs) this does not hold.

3.5 Evaluation

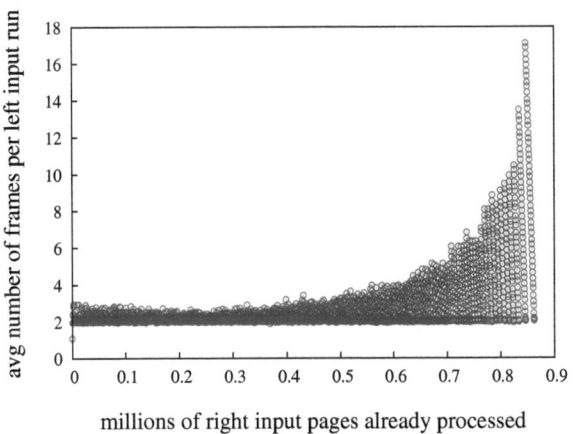

Figure 3.26: Average number of buffer pool frames per left input run during the join phase of g-join when omitting buffer pool growth limitation (scale 750)

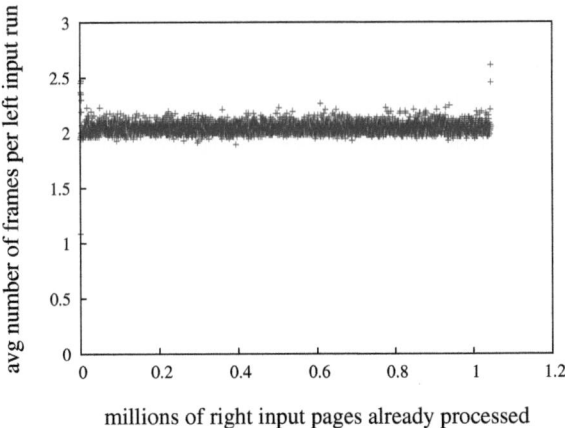

Figure 3.27: Average number of buffer pool frames per left input run during the join phase of g-join when skipping processing of the first and last right input run and omitting buffer pool growth limitation (scale 750)

3.6 G-Join Relatives: G-Distinct and G-Aggregation

Besides joins, grouping operations are of great importance in database systems. Traditional grouping algorithms are based on hashing, sorting, or on nested-loops computations. As with joins, the optimizer chooses the least cost grouping implementation based on probably incorrect or incomplete (statistical) data and this bears the risk of mistakes, which result in poor performance. We propose g-aggregation and g-distinct, the application of the g-join concept to "group by" operations, i.e., aggregation and duplicate removal, to replace traditional grouping algorithms. They combine the advantages of sort-based grouping (exploiting sorted input and early aggregation potential) and of hash-based grouping (memory requirements only depending on output size). Furthermore, they exploit available persistent indexes as source of sorted input.

Like g-join, g-aggregation[14] for an unsorted input generates sorted runs from its input. After that, an in-memory index structure is built and maintained to hold intermediate results, e.g., sums or counts. The tuples that are present in memory form the *immediate aggregation key range*. As soon as tuples move out of the immediate aggregation key range, the final aggregated result is computed and output. A priority queue guides processing of the input pages.

G-aggregation for sorted and indexed inputs is straightforward as in both cases the input is processed in ascending sort (i.e., grouping) key order and the immediate aggregation key range thus consists of only one key at any point in time. The intermediate aggregation result is updated according to every tuple with a matching grouping key. When a tuple with a greater key appears, the aggregation result is output and a new aggregation group is created. We omit a detailed discussion of these special cases.

We present the g-aggregation algorithm and run through a detailed example. Where applicable, we briefly discuss implementation alternatives. Further, we provide a qualitative comparison of g-aggregation to hash-based and sort-based grouping algorithms.

3.6.1 Basic Algorithm

G-aggregation is based on a (partial) ordering of the data by the grouping key. If the input is already sorted (or can be read from a sorted source like a B-tree), it omits sorting and processes the input quite similar to sort-based grouping. For an unsorted input producing an output small enough to fit in main memory, g-aggregation effectively executes an in-memory hash-based grouping.

For an unsorted input resulting in an output larger than main memory, g-aggregation produces sorted runs and then traverses these runs synchronously, while maintaining intermediate aggregation results for keys within the immediate aggregation key range in an in-memory index structure. As soon as a key leaves this range, the aggregation result is computed and an output tuple is generated. Algorithm 3.7 sketches the basic processing of g-aggregation. First, sorted runs are generated from input R, at the same time already aggregating values as much as possible and creating intermediate results. Then, the runs are organized in a minimum priority queue P sorted by the highest key read so far per run. For the runs from which no page has been processed yet, the sort key is the key

---

[14]We subsume g-distinct under the term g-aggregation as it constitutes a special case: while g-aggregation combines tuples having the same key column value(s), g-distinct combines tuples of which all column values comply.

Algorithm 3.7: g-aggregation for unsorted input and output larger than memory

Data: input relation R
/* first phase: run generation   */
1 $N_R \leftarrow$ run-generation-early-aggregation(R);
   /* initialize data structures for aggregation phase   */
2 create in-memory index;
3 **foreach** $R_i, 1 \leq i \leq N_R$ **do**
4 $\quad$ $min_i \leftarrow$ minimum value on first page of R_i;
5 **end**
   /* each entry in priority queue P is a pair of sort (grouping) key sk and run identifier rid */
6 initialize priority queue P with $sk=min_i$, $rid=i$, $1 \leq i \leq N_R$;
   /* second phase: aggregation   */
7 **while** P is not empty **do**
       /* determine page to be processed next   */
8 $\quad$ $id \leftarrow P.top().rid$;
9 $\quad$ $p \leftarrow$ next page of run R_{id};
10 $\quad$ **if** p is NULL **then**
       /* run R_{id} finished   */
11 $\quad\quad$ remove entry for R_{id} from priority queue P;
12 $\quad$ **else**
13 $\quad\quad$ **foreach** entry e on p **do**
14 $\quad\quad\quad$ probe into in-memory index using e;
15 $\quad\quad\quad$ **if** match m found **then**
16 $\quad\quad\quad\quad$ aggregate(m,e);
17 $\quad\quad\quad$ **else**
18 $\quad\quad\quad\quad$ create new intermediate result entry from e;
19 $\quad\quad\quad$ **end**
20 $\quad\quad$ **end**
21 $\quad\quad$ $max \leftarrow$ maximum entry on p;
22 $\quad\quad$ update priority queue P with $sk=max$, $rid=id$;
23 $\quad$ **end**
24 **end**

of the first tuple. The priority queue corresponds to priority queue C of g-join. During the aggregation phase, pages of the runs are processed in the order given by the priority queue. Each tuple e is used to probe into the in-memory index. If a match is found, the intermediate tuple in the index and the current tuple are aggregated. The **aggregate** method depends on the concrete grouping function. For example, for *count*, the group's counter is incremented, for *min*, the minimum value in the intermediate tuple is compared to the current tuple and updated if needed. We present a few examples in Section 3.6.2. After having processed all tuples on the input page, the priority queue is updated with the last processed key value for the current run.

3.6.2 Algorithm Details

The g-aggregation algorithms adopts the concept of g-join of generating sorted runs and traversing them synchronously to find matching tuples. Different grouping functions like *count*, *sum*, *avg*, *min*, *max*, and also *distinct* are basically computed in the same way. Tuples are brought together based on their grouping key and only one value per group is returned. Compared to g-join, g-aggregation allows for a more efficient run generation and requires an explicit output generation.

Run Generation with Early Aggregation

In the run generation phase, we employ replacement selection using weak-heaps and poor man's normalized keys. We refer to Section 3.3.2 for a detailed discussion of the run generation alternatives load-sort-store and replacement selection and the benefits of normalized keys.

By generating runs sorted by the grouping key in the first phase, tuples having the same key are naturally grouped within each run so that early aggregation applies. We implement early aggregation as described by Yan and Larson (1994) and before by Bitton and DeWitt (1983) for duplicate removal. Thereby, intermediate records containing the grouping key as well as an intermediate result are stored in the in-memory heap. New tuples are either combined with already existing groups according to the grouping function or – if no group with the same key is found – initiate the creation of a new group. By early aggregation, the intermediate result may be significantly reduced, i.e., run generation results in less and shorter runs. This leads to less I/O for writing and reading the sorted runs and also reduces the number of in-memory index updates during the aggregation phase.

Different Grouping Functions

In the second phase, the partial aggregation results in each run are further aggregated using the in-memory index structure. This means, intermediate tuples are used to build and probe the index structure. Depending on the concrete grouping function, intermediate tuples have different formats and must allow for (1) storing multiple computed values per group (e.g., sum and count of column values when computing *avg*, or multiple aggregated values for the same key as in

```
SELECT O_C_ID, count(O_ID), sum(O_OL_CNT)
FROM Order
GROUP BY O_C_ID
```

counting the number of orders per customer and summing up the counts of orderlines, e.g., to compute the average number of items per order) and (2) handling changing sizes of aggregates (e.g., when computing *min* on string values).

We implement the in-memory index structure as a hash table using the memory format shown in Figure 3.28. The hash table slots contain 32-bit pointers (in form of offsets) to intermediate tuples stored in the data area. Whenever a new intermediate tuple is created, memory is allocated in the data area, the tuple is copied to the newly allocated memory slot, and a pointer is stored in the hash table slot. Collisions are handled using chaining: When a tuple t_2 collides with an already stored tuple t_1, the pointer to t_1 is copied from the hash table slot to the next field of t_2 and the pointer to t_2 is stored in the hash table slot. When an output tuple is generated and removed from the hash table, the memory slot in the data area is released again. As frequent insertions and deletions might lead to a high fragmentation, we propose to compactify the data area at regular intervals or depending on the fragmentation level.

Our implementation naturally supports intermediate tuple formats containing more than one aggregated value as well as aggregates of varying size. The examples in Figure 3.28 show that the intermediate tuple format can be chosen arbitrarily. For grouping

3.6 G-Join Relatives: G-Distinct and G-Aggregation

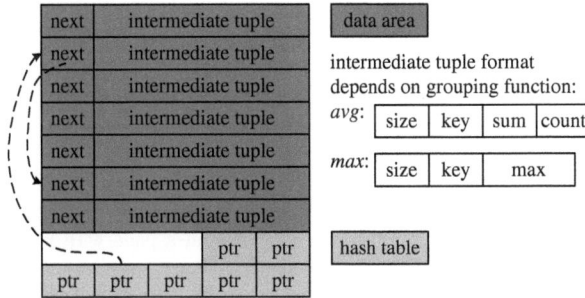

Figure 3.28: Representation of the hash table index structure: by separating the hash table from the actual data, even variable size intermediate tuple formats (as needed for grouping functions like *max*) are supported

functions with changing intermediate tuple sizes like *min* and *max* on strings, a new memory slot is allocated and the old one is released when the size of an intermediate tuple changes.

Probe Index

For g-aggregation, the same considerations regarding the in-memory index structures as discussed for g-join in Section 3.3.2 hold. However, as opposed to join processing, only one input is used to build and probe the index structure, one page at a time. In particular, each input page is read into the buffer pool only once during the aggregation phase. Thus, output generation is not triggered by the eviction of pages from the buffer pool, but must be invoked explicitly.

We sketch how this can be done for two alternatives for the in-memory probe index (and aggregation) structure: (1) a hash table as used for g-join and (2) a B-tree as representative for a sort-based index structure.

Hash table. When using a hash table, there are two possibilities to produce output tuples: One possibility is to scan the hash table at regular intervals and produce output tuples for keys which have already left the immediate aggregation key range. This enables a nearly sorted output but incurs the overhead of checking every hash table slot for outdated keys. Another possibility is to produce the output tuples in a "lazy" way, i.e., whenever an insert collision occurs, one can check if the already stored key is outdated. If yes, an output tuple is produced and its space is freed for the new key. When there are no more input tuples, the hash table is scanned a last time to output the remaining tuples. This, of course, produces unsorted output, however, the overhead for producing output tuples is small. Note that the hash table can overflow because outdated tuples are not removed (if they do not cause collisions). In this case, we need to free some space in the hash table by an intermediate scan.

B-tree. The advantage of using a B-tree as index structure is that the output is naturally produced (completely) sorted and the cost for producing the output depends only on the

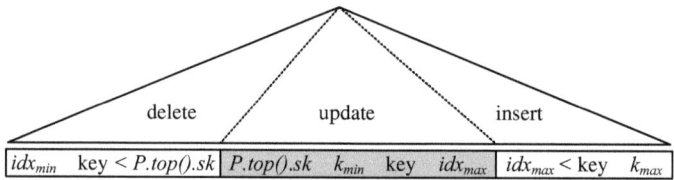

Figure 3.29: B-tree index structure: when processing a page with key values between k_{min} and k_{max}, the left part of the B-tree containing key values smaller than $P.top().sk$ can be discarded as future key values will be greater or equal; for all key values between k_{min} and the current maximum key value in the index idx_{max}, the existing intermediate tuples are extended; and for all new key values between idx_{max} and k_{max}, new intermediate tuples are created

output size and not on the index structure size. By scanning the leaf level from left to right until the immediate aggregation key range is reached, only already completely aggregated tuples are considered. In contrast to that, all intermediate and final aggregation tuples are considered when scanning the hash table. Figure 3.29 illustrates the relationship between the key value range on the currently processed page and the B-tree index structure updates.

3.6.3 Example

Figures 3.30 and 3.31 illustrate the two phases of g-aggregation computing *count*: For run generation in Figure 3.30, a priority queue of size six is used. Note that the tuples within the priority queue and the generated runs are already intermediate tuples consisting of a key and an aggregate value (or more values, depending on the grouping function). In our example, the input consists of pages (rectangles) holding five unordered tuples each. The input tuples consist of the aggregation (= sort) key and payload data of which the values are preceded by "t". Intermediate tuples consist of the aggregation key and a (partially

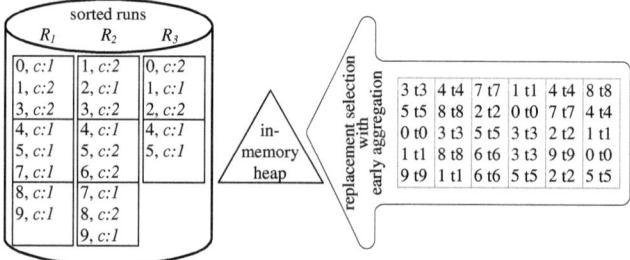

Figure 3.30: G-aggregation *count* example: run generation using replacement selection with early aggregation in a heap of size two pages, i.e., six intermediate tuples

3.6 G-Join Relatives: G-Distinct and G-Aggregation

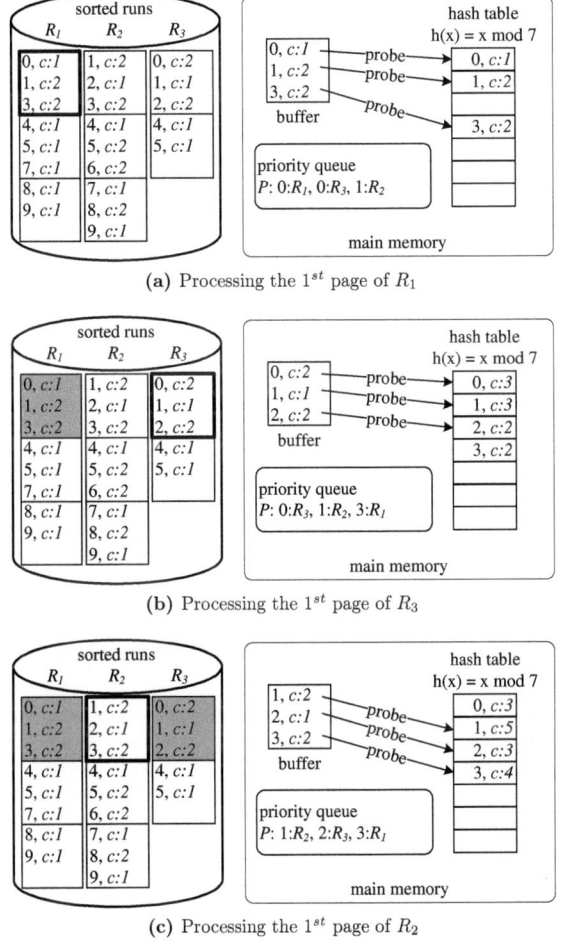

Figure 3.31: G-aggregation *count* example: aggregation phase

computed) count value which is preceded by "*c:*" and marked in italics.

During the aggregation phase, only one buffer frame is needed to process pages of the runs, the rest of the available memory is dedicated to the in-memory index structure, which we illustrate as a hash table in the example. The currently processed page is framed thickly, already processed pages are shaded. For each value on the currently processed page, the hash table is probed. When processing the first page of R_1 in Figure 3.31a, no match is found and for each tuple an intermediate record is created in the hash table. Subsequently, the priority queue P is updated and the first page of R_3 is loaded into the buffer pool. In the second step shown in Figure 3.31b, for the keys 0 and 1, an intermediate record is found in the hash table and the count values are summed up. For the key 2,

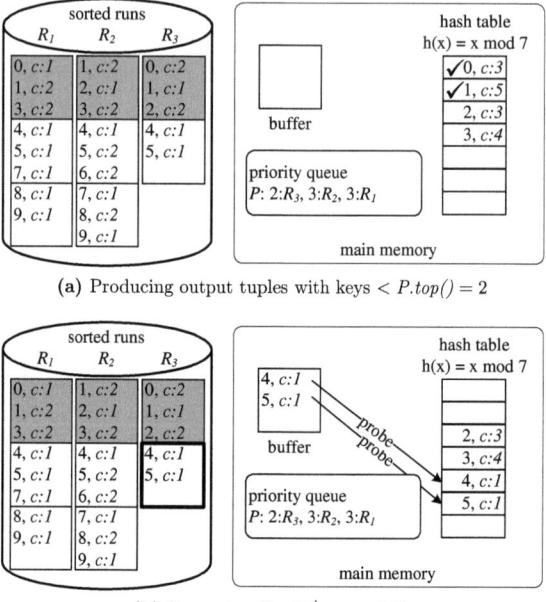

Figure 3.32: G-aggregation *count* example: aggregation phase (cont'd)

a new intermediate record is created. Then, the priority queue is updated and the third step in Figure 3.31c proceeds in the same way. In Figure 3.32a, the first output tuples for the keys 0 and 1 are produced. As future keys will be greater or equal to the top entry of the priority queue, the counts for keys less than 2 are completely computed and their records can be removed from the hash table. Note that the aggregate for the key value 0 could have been output also before processing step 3. As discussed in the previous section, there are several strategies for generating output, which do not necessarily produce the output as early as possible. In step four in Figure 3.32b, the first two hash table slots are freed again and new intermediate records are created for the keys 4 and 5.

3.6.4 Traditional Grouping Algorithms

We briefly present the traditional hash-based and sort-based grouping algorithms and summarize the main characteristics of g-aggregation in comparison to them.

Hash-based Grouping

Hash-based grouping maintains a hash table in memory, in which the output is built. The input is read tuple by tuple (page by page), probing with each one into the hash table. If a matching group is found, the tuple is added to the group (which may involve, e.g., incrementing a counter in case of *count* or comparing the group result with the current tuple and possibly replacing the group result in case of *max*). If no matching tuple is

3.6 G-Join Relatives: G-Distinct and G-Aggregation 93

found, a new hash table entry is created. If the output exceeds the memory size, the current hash table content as well as all future input tuples are partitioned. Hash-based grouping cannot exploit presorted input and produces output only after the last input tuple has been processed.

Sort-based Grouping

Sort-based grouping first sorts its input by producing sorted runs (using, e.g., quicksort or replacement selection) and then merging the runs until only one run remains. During run generation, optimizations like early aggregation are applicable and result in smaller intermediate results and thus less I/O operations during run generation and merge phase. Replacement selection is preferable to load-sort-store alternatives because it produces longer and thus fewer runs, which may be critical for the number of merge steps.[15] If the input is already sorted, the (expensive) sort phase can be omitted. The sorted input is then iterated and tuples are aggregated in a group as long as the key value does not change. Every time the key value changes, an output tuple is produced. Sort-based grouping requires only little memory (the current tuple/page as well as the current group) and processing. Further, it produces result tuples right from the start.

3.6.5 Summary and Comparison

Hash-based grouping profits from a small number of distinct values as the output size determines the efficiency of the algorithm. The larger the reduction factor, i.e., the ratio of input tuple count and output tuple count, the less memory is required and caching can be exploited. However, hash-based algorithms cannot profit from sorted inputs. Further, output can only be produced after the last input tuple is processed.

Sort-based grouping profits from presorted inputs. It can exploit early aggregation during the sort phase, but if the number of distinct values is large, then the benefit is small and the costs of sorting are very high (reading and writing the input twice or possibly even more often depending on the number of merge levels). During the aggregation phase, output is produced immediately and in sorted order.

G-aggregation generates sorted runs and then traverses the runs in sort order and computes the grouping result for the distinct values in an in-memory index. For input with a large reduction factor, g-aggregation profits from small memory requirements and caching like hash-based grouping. If the input is sorted, run generation can be omitted. If the input is roughly presorted, run generation is assumed to result in only one run, which can be processed as in sort-based grouping. During run generation, early aggregation is applicable. Further, first output results can be produced early when the respective values leave the immediate aggregation key range. Thus, g-aggregation shares the advantages of sort-based aggregation.

Table 3.9 briefly summarizes the characteristics of g-aggregation as well as those of the traditional sort-based and hash-based grouping algorithms.

We conclude that g-aggregation is competitive in the common cases (i.e., if the reduction factor is significant: sort-based grouping profits from early aggregation and hash-based grouping profits from a relatively small output) and is superior to the traditional

---

[15]Let M be the memory size and F the merge fan-in (which is approximately M). If the number of runs exceeds F, at least one intermediate merge step is required.

Property	Hash-based grouping	Sort-based grouping	G-aggregation
Input and output sizes	Output size determines the memory requirements and the number of required partitioning steps	Input size determines the number of required merge steps, output size determines the effectiveness of early aggregation and thus the I/O costs of (intermediate) merge steps	Both input and output size determine the effectiveness of early aggregation, the number of resulting runs and thus the memory requirements
Input sort order	Cannot be exploited	Is exploited	Is exploited
Duplication skew	Practically no impact	Is exploited by early aggregation during run generation	Is exploited by early aggregation during run generation
Distribution skew	Practically no impact in HyPer/dbcore as partitioning employs hash values and is adaptive w.r.t. their ranges	Practically no impact	Impact on hash table fill factor if key value ranges per page of few runs are very large
Memory requirements	Uses all available memory during grouping	Uses all available memory during run generation; during the merge phase, memory requirements depend on the number of runs; during the aggregation phase, only one page is required	Uses all available memory during run generation; during the aggregation phase, memory requirements depend on the output size within the immediate aggregation key range
Output	Unsorted	Sorted	Nearly sorted

Table 3.9: Characteristics of traditional hash-based grouping, traditional sort-based grouping, and g-aggregation

algorithms in unfavorable cases (i.e., when the reduction factor is close to 1: sort-based grouping performance is influenced mainly by the I/O costs for run generation and merge steps while hash-based grouping suffers from overflow and partitioning).

3.7 Summary and Conclusions

Query optimization in relational database systems relies on estimated query execution costs to determine a good execution plan. However, the estimates may be orders of magnitude off the real values due to outdated statistics or a poor optimization level. This results in wrong optimizer choices, e.g., regarding join algorithms, and thus in poor query execution performance.

In order to eliminate the need for possibly wrong optimizer decisions, a new robust join algorithm has been proposed by Graefe (2012) to replace the traditional algorithms based on hashing, sorting, and indexes. G-join combines elements of hash join and sort-merge join and inherits the advantages of both – it exploits different input sizes like hash join and it exploits sorted inputs like sort-merge join. Further, it exploits persistent indexes like index nested-loops join. If both inputs are sorted, g-join effectively executes a merge join. If one of the inputs fits in memory, g-join effectively executes an in-memory hash join and thus does not incur intermediate I/O. G-join permits role reversal after run generation and thus is not prone to wrong estimates of relation sizes by the query optimizer.

This work is the first to completely implement and integrate g-join into a database system. Our experimental evaluation on the modern database system HyPer/dbcore shows that g-join is competitive to hash join on unsorted data (Figure 3.14) and to sort-merge join on roughly sorted data (Figure 3.15). If there exist persistent indexes, g-join uses them like index nested-loops join but additionally profits from the rough sort order of the probe input produced by run generation (Figure 3.19). For large unsorted inputs, g-join is more robust than hash join as it does not suffer from mistaken optimizer estimates and it executes the join faster than sort-merge join as it avoids the costly complete merge of sorted runs (Figure 3.16). Our hybrid g-join implementation allows for an adaptive memory partitioning for immediate join processing and run generation. It is effective in producing first join results early and in saving I/O, thereby smoothing the performance decrease when the smaller input's size slightly exceeds memory (Figure 3.18). Duplication and distribution skew in the large input do not affect the performance of g-join. However, skew in the small input was harmful in our experiments if a hash table was chosen as in-memory index structure. Alternative sort-based in-memory index structures performed better with respect to robustness (Figure 3.22). In total, g-join performs comparable to hash join and sort-merge join for "good" cases, i.e., when optimizer decisions are appropriate, and proves its superiority for the "bad" cases, i.e., when the optimizer fails. It exploits persistent indexes like index nested-loops join. We further analyzed the memory footprint of g-join in comparison to hash join and sort-merge join and found that g-join requires the least main memory (Table 3.7). Thus, g-join improves the robustness of query processing performance without reducing query execution performance.

The concept of g-join is applicable to grouping and duplicate elimination. The g-aggregation and g-distinct algorithms profit from a (roughly) sorted input like sort-based grouping and from a large reduction factor like hash-based grouping. By generating sorted runs, the immediate aggregation key range is kept small compared to hash-based algorithms. First results are produced early as by sort-based algorithms. Thus, g-aggregation promises to be competitive to sort-based and hash-based grouping.

Chapter 4

Massively Parallel Sort-Merge Joins

Scalability in analytical query processing can be achieved by scaling the available infrastructure either horizontally (scale out) or vertically (scale up). For scale out, additional nodes are included in the infrastructure. By aggregating the computing power of hundreds of low-cost commodity systems, high performance comparable to that of supercomputers can be achieved. The widely used MapReduce framework introduced by Dean and Ghemawat (2004) builds on this mode of scaling. Scale up, by contrast, relates to the upgrade of a single node by adding or replacing resources. We focus on the latter as we believe that two emerging hardware trends will dominate the database system technology in the near future: increasing main memory capacities of several TB per server and massively parallel multi-core processing. This development demands for the revision of the algorithmic and control techniques in current database technology, which were devised specifically for disk-based systems where I/O dominates the performance.

In this chapter, we take a new look at the well-known sort-merge join, which, so far, has not been in the focus of research in scalable massively parallel multi-core data processing as it was deemed inferior to hash joins. We devise a suite of new massively parallel sort-merge (MPSM) join algorithms that are based on partial partition-based sorting. We cover a disk-based highly parallel join algorithm (D-MPSM) and a range-partitioned NUMA-affine main memory join algorithm (P-MPSM). Furthermore, we detail the skew resilience of MPSM, which offers predictable performance irrespective of the input data distribution. An extensive experimental evaluation on a modern 32-core machine with 1 TB of main memory proves the competitive performance of MPSM on large main memory databases with billions of objects. It scales almost linearly in the number of employed cores and clearly outperforms competing hash join proposals. Finally, we investigate the applicability of MPSM for non-inner join computations and in complex query plans.

Parts of the work presented in this chapter appeared in Albutiu et al. (2012a), Albutiu et al. (2012b), and Albutiu et al. (2013).

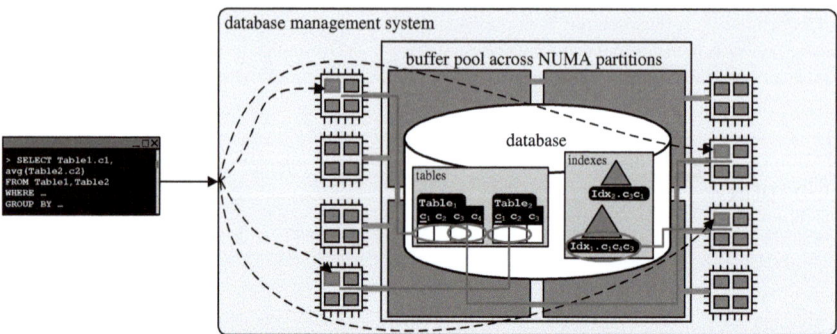

Figure 4.1: Execution of an analytical query on a multi-core NUMA system: multiple cores are working concurrently on (partly overlapping) parts of the database across the NUMA partitions

4.1 Introduction

Increasing main memory capacities of up to several TB per server and highly parallel processing exploiting multi-core architectures dominate today's hardware environments and will shape database system technology in the near future. New database software has to be carefully targeted against the upcoming hardware developments. This is particularly true for main memory database systems that try to exploit the two main hardware trends – increasing RAM capacity and core numbers. Simply porting existing algorithms to parallel environments and main memory databases may result in totally unbalanced load, in particular when the underlying architecture exhibits non-uniform memory access (NUMA). This leads to suboptimal and unpredictable execution times. Figure 4.1 illustrates the parallel processing of an analytical query on a multi-core NUMA system. Multiple threads are working concurrently on parts of the query. Each of the threads is assigned to a processing core and, thereby, to a NUMA partition. However, the threads may access data across the complete buffer pool, i.e., within all NUMA partitions. Furthermore, they may access overlapping parts of the data, which requires synchronization. In this scenario, in order to take advantage of the large buffer pool and the high parallelism, database algorithms must be designed with care. The processing work needs to be divided equally between the workers, varying data access delays have to be taken into consideration, and the requirements for synchronization between the workers should be minimized.

So far, main memory database systems were either designed for transaction processing applications, e.g., VoltDB LLC (2010), or for pure OLAP query processing like MonetDB by Boncz et al. (2009). However, the upcoming requirements for so-called real-time or operational business intelligence demand complex query processing in "real-time" on main-memory-resident data. SAP's Hana by Färber et al. (2011) and the hybrid OLTP&OLAP database system HyPer by Kemper and Neumann (2011), for which the presented massively parallel join algorithms were developed, are two such databases. The query processing of in-memory database systems is no longer I/O-bound and, therefore, it makes sense to investigate massive intra-operator parallelism in order to exploit the multi-core hardware effectively. Only query engines relying on intra-query and intra-operator parallelism will be able to meet the instantaneous response time expectations of operational business intelligence users if large main memory databases are to be explored. Single-threaded query execution is not promising to meet the high expectations of these database users as the hardware developers are no longer concerned with speeding up individual CPUs but rather concentrate on multi-core parallelization.

Consequently, we develop a new sort-based parallel join method that scales (almost) linearly with the number of cores. Thereby, on modern multi-core servers, our sort-based join outperforms hash-based parallel join algorithms, which formed the basis for multi-core optimization in recent proposals. The well-known radix join algorithm of MonetDB introduced in Manegold et al. (2002) pioneered the new focus on *cache locality* by repeatedly partitioning the arguments into ever smaller partitions. The recursive sub-partitioning, rather than directly partitioning into small fragments, preserves TLB cache locality by restricting the random write of the partitioning phase to a small number of pages whose addresses fit into the TLB cache. The join is carried out on small cache-sized fragments of the build input in order to avoid cache misses during the probe phase. Because of this cache-affine behavior, the radix join became the basis for most of the work on multi-core parallel join implementations, e.g., by Kim et al. (2009) and He et al. (2008). In addition to the cache locality, He et al. (2008) and Kim et al. (2009) also focused on low synchronization overhead and avoidance of dynamic memory allocation. Both aspects were achieved by computing histograms of the data to be partitioned and then deriving the prefix sums to determine the exact array positions into which parallel threads write their partitioned data. Unfortunately, merely relying on straightforward partitioning techniques to maintain cache locality and to keep all cores busy will not suffice for the modern hardware that scales main memory via non-uniform memory access. Besides the multi-core parallelization, the RAM and cache hierarchies also have to be taken into account. In particular, the NUMA division of the RAM has to be considered carefully. The whole NUMA system logically divides into multiple nodes, which can access both local and remote memory resources. However, a node can access its own local memory faster than remote memory, i.e., memory which is local to another node. The key to scalable high performance is **data placement** and **data movement** such that threads / cores work mostly on local data – called NUMA-friendly data processing.

To back up this claim, Figure 4.2 shows the results of a few micro-benchmarks we ran on a 1 TB main memory machine with 32 cores[16]. We therefore instantiated 32 threads to work on one relation with a total of $1600M$ ($M = 2^{20}$) tuples, each consisting of a 64-bit sort key and a 64-bit payload, in parallel. (1) We first chunked the relation and sorted the chunks of $50M$ tuples each as runs in parallel. In the "green" NUMA-affine benchmark, the sorting of each core was performed in the local NUMA RAM partition, whereas in the unfavorable "red" case, the sort was performed on a globally allocated array. We observe a severe performance penalty of a factor of three if NUMA boundaries are ignored. (2) We then analyzed the performance penalty of fine-grained synchronization. For this, the 32 threads partitioned the global relation into 32 chunks each being stored as an array. In the "red" experiment, the next write position was individually read from a (test-and-set) synchronized index variable of the corresponding partition array. In the "green" experiment, all threads were allocated precomputed sub-partitions that could be

---

[16]The system configuration is given in Section 4.6.

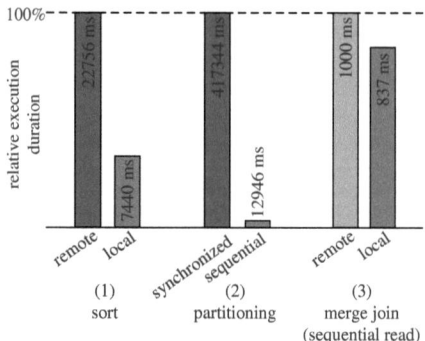

Figure 4.2: Impact of NUMA-affine versus NUMA-agnostic data processing

written sequentially without synchronization. This experiment proves that fine-grained synchronization (even with wait-free test-and-set variables) is a "no-go" for scalable data processing. (3) Finally, in the last micro-benchmark, we analyzed the tolerable performance penalty of sequentially scanning remote memory in comparison to local memory. Each of the 32 parallel threads merge-joins two chunks of $50M$ tuples each. One of the runs is local, the second run is either in remote ("yellow") or local ("green") NUMA partitions. The negative impact of the second chunk being accessed remotely compared to the second chunk being local, too, is mitigated by the hardware prefetcher as the accesses are sequential. We thus conclude that sequential scans of remote memory are acceptable from a performance perspective.

These observations and further micro-benchmarks led us to state the following three rather simple and obvious rules (called "commandments") for NUMA-affine scalable multi-core parallelization:

C1 *Thou shalt not write thy neighbor's memory randomly* – chunk the data, redistribute, and then sort / work on your data locally.

C2 *Thou shalt read thy neighbor's memory only sequentially* – let the prefetcher hide the remote access latency.

C3 *Thou shalt not wait for thy neighbors* – don't use fine-grained latching or locking and avoid synchronization points of parallel threads.

By design, the massively parallel sort-merge join algorithms (called MPSM) obey all three commandments, whereas the previously proposed hash join variants violate at least one of the commandments and, therefore, exhibit scalability problems of various forms.

We will show that the carefully engineered NUMA-friendly MPSM exhibits an outstanding performance when compared to the Wisconsin hash join by Blanas et al. (2011) and Vectorwise by Inkster et al. (2011). Our performance evaluation proves the scalability of MPSM for very large main memory databases with hundreds of GB data volume. For large numbers of cores (up to 32), MPSM outperforms the recently proposed hash-based Wisconsin join by up to an order of magnitude. MPSM scales (almost) linearly in the number of cores and, compared to the TPC-H endorsed "world champion" query processor Vectorwise, even achieves a factor of four.

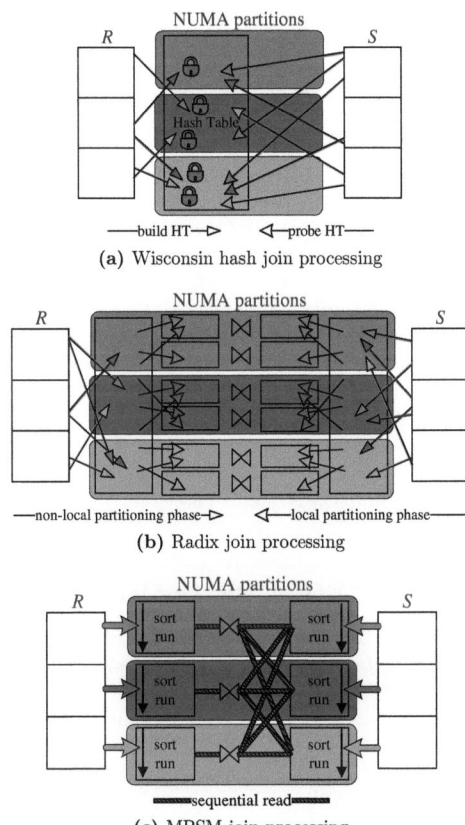

Figure 4.3: Comparison of basic join processing of Wisconsin hash join, radix join, and MPSM

4.2 A Family of MPSM Algorithms

We will first present the very basic idea of the NUMA-affine MPSM in comparison to the Wisconsin hash join and the radix join. Then we sketch the abstract algorithm and present two derived implementations for disk-based and in-memory scenarios.

The recently proposed Wisconsin hash join by Blanas et al. (2011) is based on a global shared hash table, which has to be built across the NUMA partitions by a large number of threads as sketched in Figure 4.3a. The concurrent accesses to a single hash table need synchronization via latches. Therefore, during the parallel build phase, "commandments" C2 and C3 are violated. During the probe phase, random reads to the hash table are performed across the NUMA memory partitions, which again violates C2 as the hardware prefetcher cannot hide the access latency. We illustrate the random writes and reads within the NUMA partitions using different-colored arrows and the required synchronization with locks.

The radix join of MonetDB as described in Manegold et al. (2002) and employed by Kim et al. (2009) writes across NUMA partitions during the initial partitioning phase as illustrated in Figure 4.3b. The radix join repeatedly partitions the arguments in order to achieve cache locality of the hash table probes despite their random nature. Unfortunately, the price for this locality is the partitioning of both join arguments across the NUMA memory during the first partitioning step, which violates C2.

Our massively parallel sort-merge (MPSM) join is designed to take NUMA architectures into account, which were not yet in the focus of prior work on parallel join processing for main memory systems. As illustrated in Figure 4.3c, each data chunk is processed, i.e., sorted, locally, which conforms to C1. Unlike traditional sort-merge joins, we refrain from merging the sorted runs to obtain a global sort order and rather join them all in a brute-force but highly parallel manner. We opt to invest more into scanning in order to avoid the hard to parallelize merge phase. Obviously, this decision does not result in a globally sorted join output but exhibits a partial sort order that allows for sort order based subsequent operations, e.g, early aggregation. During the join phase, data accesses across NUMA partitions are sequential as required by C2, so that the prefetcher mostly hides the access overhead. We do not employ shared data structures so that no expensive synchronization is required and C3 is met. Therefore, MPSM obeys all three NUMA commandments by design.

4.2.1 The Basic MPSM (B-MPSM) Algorithm

The basic MPSM (B-MPSM) algorithm is sketched in Figure 4.4 for a scenario with four worker threads. The input data is chunked into equally sized chunks among the workers, so that for instance worker W_1 is assigned a chunk R_1 of input R and another chunk S_1 of input S. In the following, we call R the private input and S the public input. Each worker sorts its data chunks, thereby generating sorted runs of the input data in parallel. These runs are not merged as doing so would heavily reduce the "parallelization power" of modern multi-core machines. After the sorting phase is finished, each worker processes only its own chunk of the private input but sequentially scans the complete public input. We will later devise the range-partitioned variant where this complete scanning is avoided to speed up the join phase even more beyond parallelization. During run generation (phase 1 and phase 2), each worker thread handles an equal share of both the public and the private input. These phases do not require any synchronization between the workers

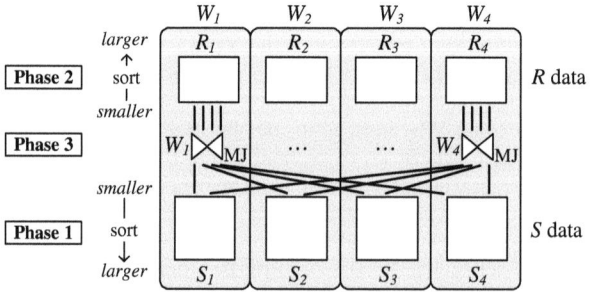

Figure 4.4: B-MPSM join with four workers W_i

4.2 A Family of MPSM Algorithms

and are performed in local memory, which we have shown to be advantageous for the sort operator in the micro-benchmarks in Figure 4.2. Even if data has to be copied from remote to local chunks, this can be amortized by carrying out the first partitioning step of sorting while copying. In phase 3, each worker joins its sorted private input run with the sorted public input runs using merge join. The join phase requires reading non-local memory, however, only sequentially. As we have shown before, sequential scans heavily profit from (implicit processor) prefetching and cache locality and therefore do not affect performance significantly.

The B-MPSM algorithm is absolutely skew resistant and obeys the three "commandments" for NUMA-affine design we stated above: During the run generation phases for public and private input, only local memory is written. In the join phase, all runs (local and remote) are scanned sequentially. Furthermore, B-MPSM requires only one synchronization point as we need to make sure that the public input runs S_i are ready before we start the join phase. Note that the sort phase of the private data R need not be finished before other threads start their join phase. Thus, the synchronization is limited to ensure that all other workers have finished their sorting of the public input chunk before phase 3 (join) is entered. The fact that the output of each worker is a sorted run may be leveraged by subsequent operators like sort-based aggregation. Also, presorted relations can obviously be exploited to omit one or both sorting phases.

B-MPSM basically executes w sort-merge joins in parallel, where w is the number of worker threads. In each of these sort-merge joins, $1/w^{\text{th}}$ of the input relations is processed. A crude complexity approximation per worker W_i results in:

$$
\begin{array}{rl}
& |S|/w \cdot log(|S|/w) \quad \text{sort chunk } S_i \text{ of size } |S|/w \\
+ & |R|/w \cdot log(|R|/w) \quad \text{sort chunk } R_i \text{ of size } |R|/w \\
+ & w \cdot |R|/w \quad \text{process run } R_i \text{ for all } S \text{ runs} \\
+ & w \cdot |S|/w \quad \text{process all } S \text{ runs} \\
= & |S|/w \cdot log(|S|/w) + |R|/w \cdot log(|R|/w) + |R| + |S|
\end{array}
$$

On the bottom line, each thread sorts "its" chunks of R and S and processes all sorted S runs. Thereby, the own R run is read w times as each of the S runs possibly joins with the local run.

The formula above reveals that the sort phases of B-MPSM scale well with the number of worker threads w. The join phase, however, requires each worker to process the complete public input regardless of the processing parallelism given. For I/O-bound disk-based processing, this is hidden by the I/O latency. However, for pure in-memory processing, we address this issue by preprocessing the private input data so that much of the work during the join phase can be saved.

So far, we presented the basic concept of MPSM, which (in object-oriented terminology) is only an abstract class for several algorithmic specializations. We present two derived implementations:

(P-MPSM) ← ⌈ B-MPSM ⌉ → (D-MPSM)

P-MPSM is a pure main memory version that range-partitions the input data, thereby providing scalability with respect to processing cores. D-MPSM is a RAM-constrained version that spools runs to disk. Both scenarios are common in main memory database systems and require attention when database operators are designed. We carefully consider both variants detailed enough to allow for an implementation and considerations

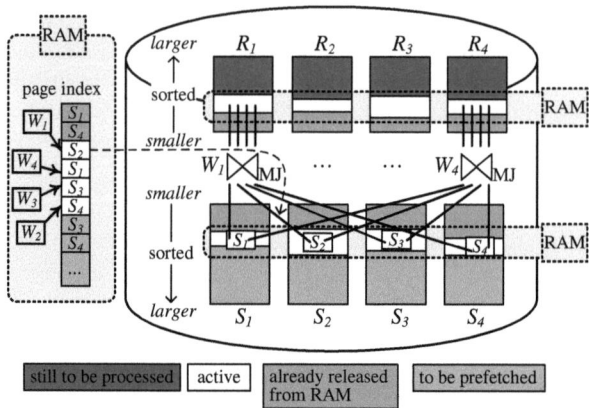

Figure 4.5: Disk-enabled MPSM join: the four workers W_i progress synchronously through their R_i run and all S runs, thereby only active parts of the runs are in RAM

about performance. For the rest of the chapter, we then focus on the range-partitioned main memory version and use the terms P-MPSM and MPSM interchangeably.

4.2.2 The Memory Constrained Disk-enabled MPSM (D-MPSM) Algorithm

The presented MPSM can effectively be adapted to scenarios, in which the intermediate result data is too large to be kept in main memory. Even in main memory database systems like HyPer that retain the entire transactional database in RAM, the query processor spools intermediate results to disk to preserve the precious RAM capacity for the transactional working set. Therefore, it is important to support both pure main memory algorithms and a disk-based processing mode with a very small RAM footprint.

The disk-enabled MPSM (D-MPSM) processes the left and right input runs by synchronously moving through the key domain, which is sorted. The resulting data locality allows to spill already processed data to disk and to prefetch data that is to be processed soon. Figure 4.5 illustrates the approach: Both R and S runs are stored on disk, only the currently processed pages (white) need to be main-memory-resident. Already processed data is not touched again and thus can be released from RAM (green). Soon to be processed S data is prefetched from disk asynchronously (yellow).

For this purpose, we maintain a page index, which is ordered pagewise by key value. The index is built during run generation and contains pairs $\langle v_{ij}, S_i \rangle$ where v_{ij} is the first (minimal) join key value on the jth page of run S_i. Figure 4.5 depicts a simplified page index (only run identifiers) on the left. It actually contains the following information:

sorted by v_{ij}							
v_{11}	v_{41}	v_{21}	v_{12}	v_{31}	v_{42}	v_{32}	v_{43}	...
S_1	S_4	S_2	S_1	S_3	S_4	S_3	S_4	...

where $v_{11} \leq v_{41} \leq \ldots \leq v_{43}$. Both the prefetcher and the workers process the S input data in the order specified by the index, thereby synchronously moving through the key domain and allowing to keep only a small part of the data in memory during join processing. All page index entries already processed by the "slowest" worker, e.g., W_1 in the illustration, point to run pages that may be released from RAM (green). The prefetcher is supposed to pre-load run pages according to the index before they are accessed by any worker (yellow). Implicitly, the workers' private input runs R_i are read from disk (red), processed, and released from RAM in ascending order of join keys. Please note that the common page index structure does not require any synchronization as it is accessed read-only.

Obviously, the performance of D-MPSM is determined by the time to write (run generation) and read (join phase) both inputs. Therefore, in order to exploit the power of multiple cores, a sufficiently large I/O bandwidth (i.e., a very large number of disks) is required.

4.2.3 The Range-Partitioned MPSM (P-MPSM) Algorithm

The range-partitioned MPSM (P-MPSM) extends the B-MPSM algorithm by a prologue phase to range-partition and assign the private input data to the workers in a way that allows saving much of the work during the join phase. The different phases of the algorithm are sketched in Figure 4.6 for a scenario with four workers, choosing R as private input and S as public input. In phase 1, the public input is chunked and sorted locally, resulting in runs S_1 to S_4. Subsequently, in phase 2, the private input is chunked into C_1 to C_4 and those chunks are range-partitioned. We employ a histogram-based technique to ensure that the range partitions are balanced even for skewed data distributions. This will be explained in detail in Section 4.4. Thereby, the private input data is partitioned into disjoint key ranges as indicated by the different shades in Figure 4.6, ranging from white over light and dark gray to black. In phase 3, each worker then sorts its private input

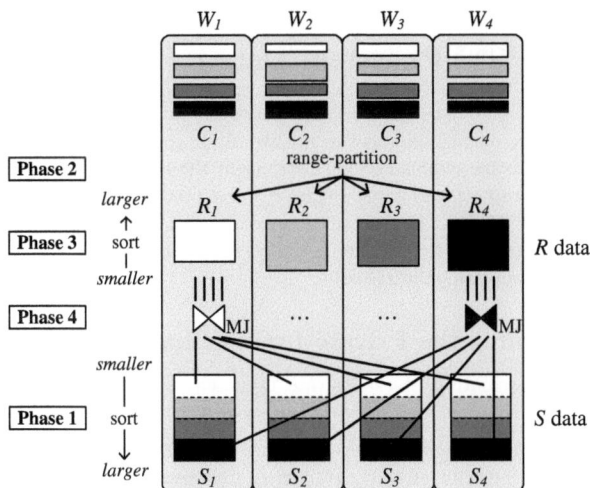

Figure 4.6: P-MPSM join with four workers W_i

chunk and, in phase 4, each worker merge-joins its own private run R_i with all public input runs S_j.

By refining the MPSM to use range-partitioning, each thread conducts only the join between $1/w^{\text{th}}$ of the join key domain of R and S. This reduces the complexity per worker W_i to:

$$\begin{array}{rl} & |S|/w \cdot log(|S|/w) \quad \text{sort chunk } S_i \text{ of size } |S|/w \\ + & |R|/w \quad \text{range-partition chunk } R_i \text{ of size } |R|/w \\ + & |R|/w \cdot log(|R|/w) \quad \text{sort chunk } R_i \text{ of size } |R|/w \\ + & w \cdot |R|/w \quad \text{process run } R_i \text{ for all } S \text{ runs} \\ + & w \cdot |S|/w^2 \quad \text{process } 1/w^{\text{th}} \text{ of each } S \text{ run} \\ = & |S|/w \cdot log(|S|/w) + |R|/w + |R|/w \cdot log(|R|/w) + |R| + |S|/w \end{array}$$

Compared to the complexity approximation of B-MPSM, range-partitioning pays off if the cost of range-partitioning R is smaller than the savings in join processing, i.e., if

$$|R|/w \leq |S| - |S|/w.$$

For a parallelism greater than or equal to two and $|R| \leq |S|$, it pays off. The performance of P-MPSM thus scales almost linearly with the number of parallel worker threads w, which is decisive for the effective multi-core scalability of P-MPSM, as our experimental evaluation will also prove.

In general, the two input relations to a join operation are not equally sized but usually consist of a larger (fact) table and smaller (dimension) tables. Assigning the private input role R to the smaller of the input relations and thus the public input role S to the larger yields the best performance. Thereby, only a small fraction (depending on the number of worker threads w) of the remote public input needs to be processed while the smaller private input is scanned several times with almost no performance penalties. We will present evaluation results quantifying the performance impact of reversed public/private input roles in Section 4.6.2.

4.3 The MPSM Phases in Detail

In this section, we present the algorithmic details of the individual P-MPSM phases. First, we cover the efficient partitioning of the private input (phase 2). Then, we present our two-phase sorting routine, which is 30% faster than the STL sort and further allows for the integration of chunking and sorting (phase 1 and phase 3). Last, we address the join phase (phase 4) of P-MPSM. In particular, we sketch an efficient search method, which allows to quickly determine the starting point of merge join within the sorted runs with a small number of compare operations.

4.3.1 Partitioning the Private Input (Phase 2)

We design the redistribution of the private input chunks C_i to be very efficient, i.e., *branch-free, comparison-free,* and *synchronization-free*.

(1) *branch-freeness* and *comparison-freeness* are achieved by using radix-clustering as introduced by Manegold et al. (2002) on the highest B bits of the join key where $log(w) \leq B$. For $log(w) = B$, radix-clustering results in exactly w clusters. By increasing B, we can account for skew in both R and S as we will discuss in Section 4.4.

4.3 The MPSM Phases in Detail

(2) We then range-partition the private input chunks, guaranteeing *synchronization-freeness* by letting each worker write sequentially to precomputed sub-partitions within all runs. For this purpose, each thread builds a histogram on its chunk of the global relation R representing the key value distribution within the chunk. The local histograms are combined to obtain a set of prefix sums where each prefix sum represents the start positions of each worker's partitions within the target runs. Each worker then scatters its input chunk to the partitions using the prefix sums and updating them accordingly. This approach was adapted from the radix join of He et al. (2008) and is also described by Cieslewicz and Ross (2008).

We demonstrate the partitioning of R in Figure 4.7 for two workers, $B = 1$, and a join key range of $[0, 32)$. Each worker thread W_i scans its own chunk C_i and probes for each tuple into a histogram array depending on its highest key bit (which we show underlined), i.e., join key values < 16 are assigned to the first position and join key values ≥ 16 are assigned to the second. After all tuples have been processed, the histograms specify the number of key values which fall into the different target partitions. According to h_1, chunk C_1 contains four entries for the first and three for the second target partition. As given by h_2, chunk C_2 contains three entries for the first and four for the second target partition. For illustration purposes, the tuples are colored white and black according to their target partition. From the combined histograms, prefix sums are computed that point to the target subpartition into which the workers scatter their chunk's tuples. For example, the prefix sum ps_1 denotes that W_1 scatters its entries for the first and second target partition starting at position 0. According to ps_2, W_2 scatters tuples belonging to the first target partition beginning at position 4 (as W_1 writes to positions 0 to 3), and those belonging to the second target partition beginning at position 3. In general, the ps-entries of worker W_i for target partitions j are computed as

$$ps_i[j] = \begin{cases} 0, & \text{if } i = 1 \\ \sum_{k=1}^{i-1} h_k[j], & \text{else.} \end{cases}$$

Actually, the ps_i contain pointers to the positions, no index values, as indicated by the dotted arrows in Figure 4.7, i.e., $ps_i[j] = \&R_j[(\sum_{k=1}^{i-1} h_k[j])]$. The prefix sums ps_i per worker W_i, which are computed from the combined local histograms, are essential for the synchronization-free parallel scattering of the tuples into their range partition. Every worker has a dedicated index range in each array R_i into which it can write sequentially. This is orders of magnitude more efficient than synchronized writing into the array – as shown in Figure 4.2 (2).

Note that depending on the actual join key value distribution, in particular the minimum and maximum join key values, it might be necessary to preprocess the join keys before applying radix-clustering. This can usually be done efficiently using bitwise shift operations. Although we use radix-clustering for partitioning the private input, the approach is not restricted to integer join keys. However, if long strings are used as join keys, MPSM should work on the hash codes of those strings, thereby giving up the meaningful sorting of the output. Furthermore, main memory database systems usually employ dictionary encoding so that joins on strings are usually internally executed as joins on integers anyway.

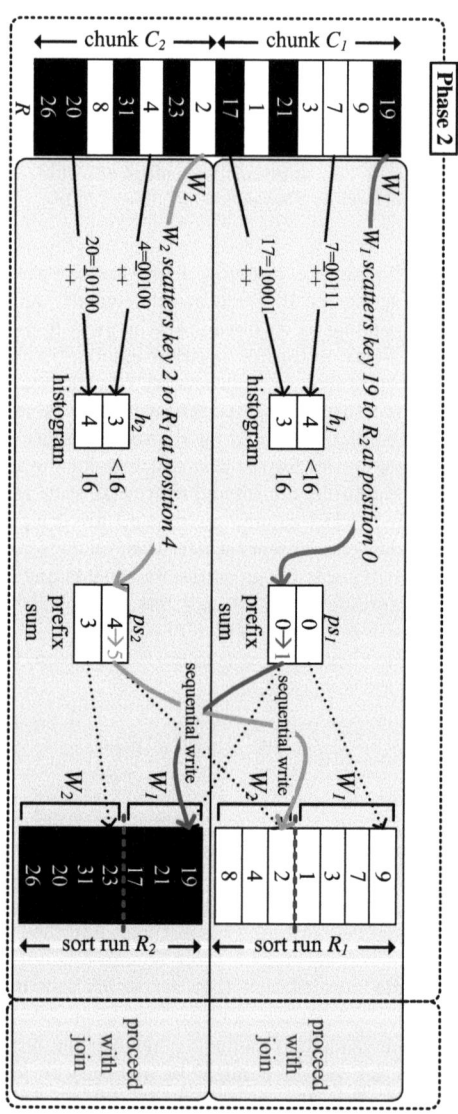

Figure 4.7: Phase 2 of P-MPSM processing 5-bit join keys in the range [0,32) and using a $B = 1$ bit histogram for creating $w = 2$ target partitions

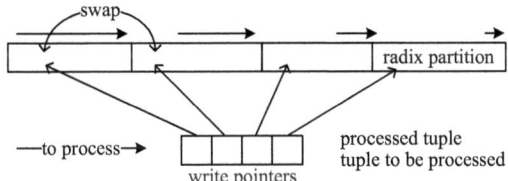

Figure 4.8: Radix sort

4.3.2 Sorting the Private and Public Inputs (Phases 1 and 3)

Efficient sorting is decisive for the performance of MPSM. As we deal with (realistic) large join keys and payloads that need to be sorted, we cannot utilize the specialized bitonic sorting routines by Chhugani et al. (2008) that exploit the SIMD registers, as these are limited to 32-bit data types. Instead, we developed our own two-phase sorting algorithm that operates as follows:

1. Recursive **in-place** radix sort (see Knuth (1973)) that (in each recursion step) generates $2^8 = 256$ partitions according to the 8 most significant bits (MSB). This works by computing a 256-bucket histogram and determining the boundaries of each partition. Then, the data elements are swapped into their partition. We illustrate one recursion step for $2^2 = 4$ partitions in Figure 4.8. The tuples are processed from left to right, i.e., beginning with the left-most partition containing the smallest key values. Tuples not yet processed are shown black, already processed tuples are shown green. When all tuples of the first partition have been processed, some of the tuples in the subsequent partitions are likely to be already at the correct position, i.e., they have already been processed. Therefore, the algorithm can omit these tuples and proceed with the first non-processed tuple. This is denoted by the arrows shown above the partitions. The number of tuples to process in each partition decreases from left to right and usually is 0 in the last partition.

2. One final insertion sort for partitions containing less than 100 elements results in the total ordering.

We analyzed that this sorting routine is about 30% faster than the STL sort method, even when up to 32 workers sort their local runs in parallel. Note that we do not employ synchronization-heavy parallel sorting. Instead, each worker sorts a separate chunk of data into a run.

The private input data is chunked and redistributed among the workers in phase 2 so that each worker's private input chunk is stored in local memory before it is sorted in phase 3. For the public input data, it might be necessary to copy the data from remote to local memory when it is chunked. We efficiently integrate the chunking of the public input with the subsequent sort phase. That way, we eliminate one complete pass through the public input data chunk. As illustrated in Figure 4.9 for an example using a fan-out of 4, i.e., 2 bits, the first step of radix sort is not conducted in-place, but is used to copy the data into the private memory of each worker. In the example, worker W_2 copies the tuples belonging to chunk S_2 into its local memory and, at the same time, conducts the first radix-partitioning phase of radix sort. The next write position within each partition is maintained as a pointer and incremented accordingly. For this purpose, each worker

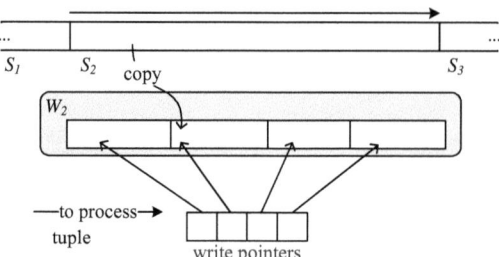

Figure 4.9: Integrated chunking and sorting: chunking is conducted as the first step of radix sort

initially builds a histogram for its data chunk and computes the prefix sum as described in detail in Section 4.3.1.

4.3.3 Join Phase (Phase 4)

Due to partitioning, the private input data chunks contain only a fraction of the key value domain and thus probably join only with a fraction of each public input data chunk. As indicated in Figure 4.6, the public input runs are therefore implicitly partitioned by the sorting order. Sequentially searching for the starting point of merge join within each public data chunk would incur numerous expensive comparisons. Thus, we determine the first public input tuple of run S_j to be joined with the private input run R_i using *interpolation search* as sketched in Figure 4.10.

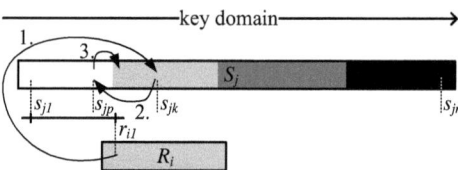

Figure 4.10: Interpolation search for r_{i1} in S_j

Depending on which of the first values of each run – s_{j1} and r_{i1} – is larger (in general this will be r_{i1} because the key range of R runs is limited while the key range of S runs is not), we search for it within the other run by iteratively narrowing the search space. The most probable position in each iteration is computed by applying the rule of proportion using the minimum and maximum index positions (1 and n for step 1. in Figure 4.10) and the minimum and maximum key values of the current search space (s_{j1} and s_{jn}), and the difference of the searched key value (r_{i1}) and the search space minimum key value (s_{j1}). The computed index per iteration is always relative to the search space starting index. In the illustration in Figure 4.10, three steps are required to find the starting point of merge join:

1. the search space is $[s_{j1}, s_{jn}]$, i.e., from indexes 1 to n, thus we compute the position $k = 1 + (n-1) \cdot {(r_{i1} - s_{j1})}/{(s_{jn} - s_{j1})}$

2. the search space is narrowed to $[s_{j1}, s_{jk}]$, i.e., from indexes 1 to k, so we compute the position $p = 1 + (k-1) \cdot (r_{i1} - s_{j1})/(s_{jk} - s_{j1})$

3. the search space is further narrowed to $[s_{jp}, s_{jk}]$, i.e., from indexes p to k, so we compute the position $p + (k-p) \cdot (r_{i1} - s_{jp})/(s_{jk} - s_{jp})$

and find the start index of the light gray partition.

4.4 Skew Resilience of P-MPSM

The basic B-MPSM as well as the disk variant D-MPSM are completely skew immune as they do not range-partition. By contrast, P-MPSM employs partitioning by key value and thus needs to consider skewed data.

So far, we discussed P-MPSM using statically determined partition bounds. In case of a uniform data distribution, the presented algorithm assigns balanced workloads (i.e., equally sized chunks) to the workers. It is important to note that the location of the data within the relations R and S – e.g., if by time-of-creation-clustering small values appear mostly before large values – has no negative effect. The *location skew* among the R and S runs is implicitly handled by range-partitioning the R data and thereby limiting the S data each worker has to process. Of course, location skew may cause slight NUMA effects that cannot be controlled lastly. As our evaluation in Section 4.6.2 shows, these effects usually have a positive impact on performance as the join partners of a partition R_i are better clustered in S.

We now present a more elaborate version of P-MPSM that can handle *distribution skew* while incurring only very little overhead to the overall performance. Skew resilience is achieved by not determining the partition bounds statically but computing them based on dynamically obtained information about the key value distributions in R and S. We exploit the sort order of the public input S to compute arbitrarily precise histograms representing the key value distribution of S en passant, i.e., in almost no time. Further, we increase the number B of bits used for the histogram computation for radix-clustering of the private input R and thereby also obtain very precise histograms representing the private input join key value distribution. We then determine global load-balancing partition bounds based on the computed distributions. We show that the presented approach adds only very little overhead to the overall join processing.

For a better illustration, we split the range-partitioning phase 2 into the following subphases: The histogram on S is determined in phase 2.1 using a cumulative distribution function (CDF). The histogram on R is determined in phase 2.2 using probing as described above but increasing the number of leading bits B used for fine-grained histogram boundaries. In phase 2.3, we combine the information about the key value distributions in R and S to find global partition bounds, called splitters, balancing the costs for sorting R chunks and joining R and S runs. That way, we ensure that each worker thread is assigned a balanced workload to make sure that they all finish at the same time, which is very important for subsequent query operators. Figure 4.11 summarizes the refined phase 2 of P-MPSM.

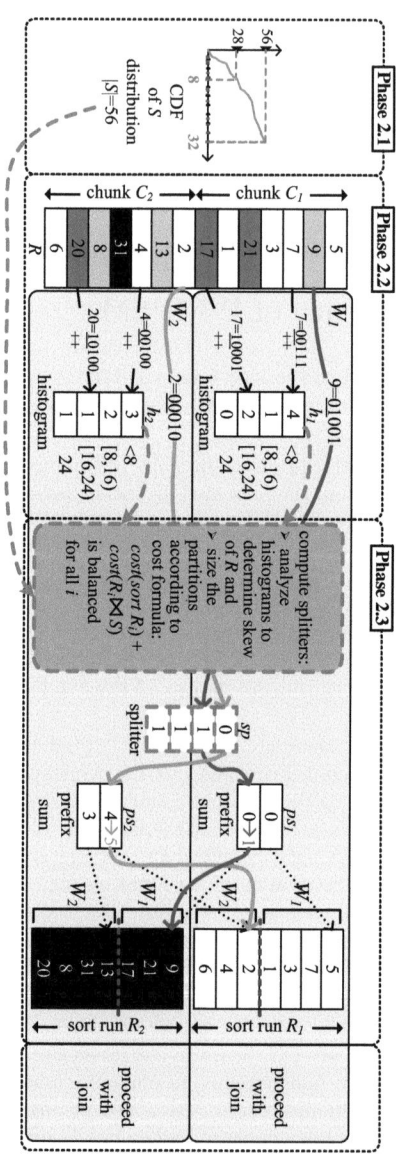

Figure 4.11: Refined phase 2 of P-MPSM: load balanced partitioning of the private input R for an example with skewed (mostly small) join keys in the range $[0, 32]$.

4.4 Skew Resilience of P-MPSM

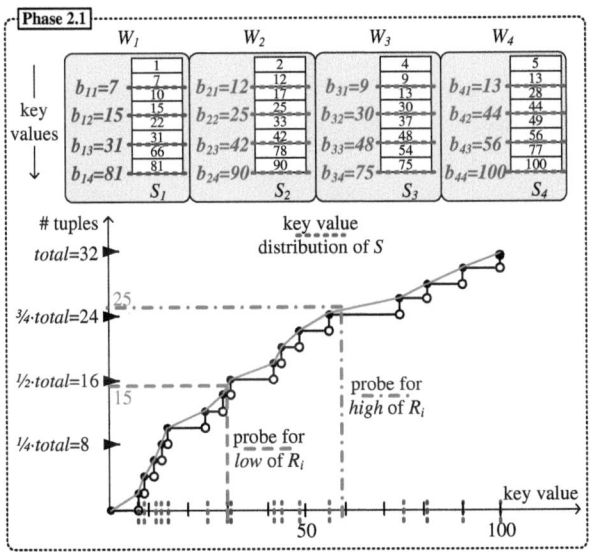

Figure 4.12: P-MPSM CDF computation: example with skewed input (mostly small key values)

4.4.1 Global S Data Distribution (Phase 2.1)

In phase 2.1, we gain insight into the global S data distribution in two steps: In the first step, each worker thread W_i computes an equi-height histogram for its local input run S_i. Building the equi-height histograms comes at almost no costs as the data is already sorted. Then, the local histograms are merged to provide a global distribution view. The procedure is exemplified in Figure 4.12 for four runs S_1 to S_4 with skewed data, i.e., small join key values occur much more often than large join key values. The local equi-height histogram bounds b_{ij} for each worker W_i computed during the first phase are marked as red dotted lines within the input runs. In the example, each worker collects four local bounds, i.e., the local histograms are of size four. In the second step, the local partition bounds of all workers are collected as input to a global cumulative distribution function (CDF). The CDF allows to efficiently determine the number of tuples in S having a key value smaller than a certain threshold. That way, the number of joining S tuples for a partition R_i can be computed by extracting the CDF values for the *high* and *low* key values of R_i (resulting in 25 and 15 in the example in Figure 4.12) and computing the difference.

Using the local equi-height histograms, we can only estimate the gradient of the step function by approximating each step to be equally high. Of course, the real global distribution deviates (slightly) from this as the different workers' equi-height partitions have overlapping key ranges. In the example in Figure 4.12, each worker thread determines $w = 4$ local bounds. In general, we propose to compute $f \cdot w$, $f \in \mathcal{N}$, local bounds per worker for a better precision. By increasing f and thus the number of local bounds determined by each worker, more fine-grained information about the global data distribution

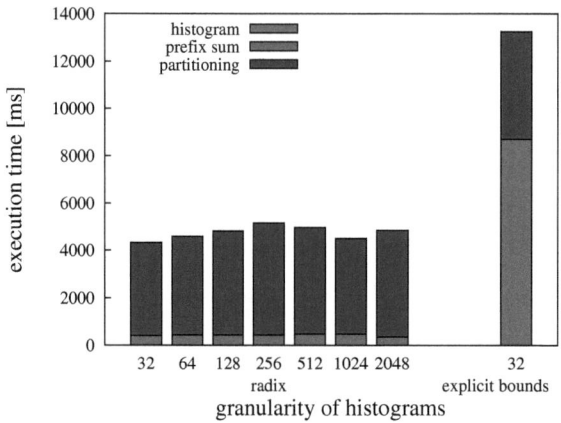

Figure 4.13: Fine-grained histograms at little overhead

can be collected at negligible costs.

Note that the CDF allows for configuration changes concerning the number of workers at runtime. Appropriate partition limits are then found using interpolation as denoted in Figure 4.12 by the diagonal connections between steps. This also allows to combine the global S data distribution represented by the CDF with the R data distribution in order to handle uncorrelated or even negatively correlated skew in R and S as we will show below.

4.4.2 Global R Data Distribution Histogram (Phase 2.2)

In phase 2.2, each worker scans its private input chunk C_i and computes a local histogram on it using radix-histogramming. The number of leading bits B used for probing determines the precision of the histogram, i.e., using B bits we obtain a histogram of size 2^B. Building a more fine-grained histogram does only incur little overhead but allows for a much more precise computation of global R bounds. By merging some of the clusters to form w partitions with a balanced workload of $cost(sort(R_i))+cost(R_i \bowtie S)$, we obtain the global partition bounds. On the left hand side of Figure 4.13, we see that higher precision of radix-histogramming comes at no additional cost. On the right hand side, we see the inferior performance of comparison-based partitioning according to explicit bounds.

In Figure 4.11, the approach is exemplified for a scenario with two workers clustering two initial chunks and redistributing them to two target partitions. They first build a local histogram of size 4 ($B = 2$) each, dividing the skewed input data with key domain $[0, 32)$ into four partitions: < 8, $[8, 16)$, $[16, 24)$, ≥ 24. The histograms reveal that the chunks contain many more small key values than large key values. In particular, there are a total of seven values in the first partition, three values in the second, three values in the third, and one value in the fourth partition.

4.4.3 Partitioning the Private Input R (Phase 2.3)

In phase 2.3, we use the global CDF for S determined in phase 2.1 and the global R distribution histogram from phase 2.2 to heuristically determine global partition bounds (called splitters) using a complexity approximation that takes into account both the sort costs of the R chunks and the join costs per worker W_i:

$$\begin{aligned}
\textit{split-relevant-cost}_i = & \\
& |R_i| \cdot log(|R_i|) && \text{sort chunk } R_i \\
+ & \quad w \cdot |R_i| && \text{process run } R_i \\
+ & \quad \text{CDF}(R_i.high) - \text{CDF}(R_i.low) && \text{process relevant } S \text{ data}
\end{aligned}$$

where $R_i.low$ and $R_i.high$ denote the radix boundaries for which we probe in the CDF. Note that, because of the sorting, S can be partitioned at any position. The boundaries are determined at the radix granularity of R's histograms.

As shown in Figure 4.12 and on the left of Figure 4.11 using blue dashed lines, the tentative R histogram bounds are used to probe into the CDF to determine the anticipated S costs for the currently considered R partition $[low, high)$. If the key values in R and S are uniformly distributed or skewed in a correlated way, the global R partition bounds will be similar to the global S partition bounds and thus all R_i will be approximately equally sized. If the key value distributions in R and S are uncorrelated, the R_i cardinalities may be very different so that we need to weight their effect on the overall performance to find the final global partition bounds.

We opt to partition R and S such that each worker is assigned the same amount of work, i.e., we determine the partition bounds such that they minimize the biggest cost $\textit{split-relevant-cost}_i$ over all $1 \leq i \leq w$. We sketch the basic splitter computation adapted from Ross and Cieslewicz (2009) in Algorithm 4.1. The splitter computation algorithm takes as inputs the cardinalities and key value distributions of R and S as well as a cost function and an upper bound for the processing cost of one partition. Further, an upper bound for the number of computed splitters is specified. The algorithm returns the computed splitters, which we use to create w partitions with equal workloads. In contrast to Ross and Cieslewicz (2009), we consider only the bucket bounds of the global R histogram as possible partition bounds and probe into the CDF to determine the corresponding S partition cardinality.

To simplify matters in the example in Figure 4.11, we assume the key value distribution of S to be correlated to that of R. Therefore, when probing into the CDF using 8 and 32 as $[low, high)$ values for R_2, those bounds divide S into equally sized partitions. Thus, according to the histograms h_1 and h_2 and the CDF of S, the first cluster containing key values < 8 becomes the first partition and the other three clusters with key values ≥ 8 form the second partition. This is denoted by the indexes 0 for the first partition and 1 for the second partition given in the splitters vector sp.

Having determined the global partition bounds, we then partition the private input chunks accordingly. As detailed in Section 4.3.1, we avoid synchronization by letting each worker write sequentially to precomputed partitions. For this purpose, the local histograms are combined to a set of prefix sums where each prefix sum ps_i represents the partitions of worker W_i within the target runs. Each worker scatters its input chunk to the partitions using the prefix sums via the indirection of the splitters vector sp, i.e., worker W_i scatters its next tuple t as follows:

$$\texttt{memcpy}(ps_i[sp[t.key \gg (64 - B)]]\texttt{++}, t, t.size)$$

Algorithm 4.1: Splitter computation based on the global R and S data distributions and the *split-relevant-cost* function (adapted from Ross and Cieslewicz (2009))

Data: cardinality of private input $|R|$, cardinality of public input $|S|$, number of splitters k, cost function *split-relevant-cost*, upper cost bound b, global R data distribution histogram H, global S data distribution CDF

1   $idx_R \leftarrow 0$;
2   $idx_S \leftarrow 0$;
3   $idx_H \leftarrow 0$;
4   $i \leftarrow 0$;
5   **while** *split-relevant-cost*$(|R| - idx_R, |S| - idx_S) > b$ **do**
6   **if** $i \geq k$ **then**
7 | return error;
8   **end**
     /* min-key(p)/max-key(p) return the lower/upper bound of partition $H[p]$ */
9   find largest q among $idx_H, \ldots, H.size - 1$ such that *split-relevant-cost*$(c_1, c_2) \leq b$ where
       $c_1 = \sum_{idx_H \leq j \leq q} H[j]$ /* number of R tuples within examined key range */
       $c_2 = CDF(max\text{-}key(q)) - CDF(min\text{-}key(idx_H))$ /* number of S tuples within examined key range */
10    $splitter[i] = max\text{-}key(q)$;
11    $i \leftarrow i + 1$;
12    $idx_H = q + 1$;
13    $idx_R = \sum_{0 \leq j \leq q} H[j]$;
14    $idx_S = CDF(max\text{-}key(q))$;
15 **end**
16 return $splitter[0], \cdots, splitter[i-1]$;

ps_i contains pointers, not indexes because each worker scatters to different arrays. According to the global R partition bounds $b_1 = 8$ and $b_2 = 32$, there are four entries of chunk C_1 falling into the first partition and three (1+2+0) falling into the second. From chunk C_2, three values belong to the first and four (2+1+1) to the second partition. The local histograms (which are computed per chunk) are combined to global prefix sums. The values in ps_1 and ps_2 denote that worker W_1 will scatter its data falling into the first partition to run R_1 beginning at position 0, whereas worker W_2 will write its data for the first partition to run R_1 beginning at position 4. The prefix sum ps_i is incremented for each tuple scattered. Please note that – depending on the key distribution in R – the resulting runs might not be of equal size. It is more important that the cost is balanced rather than the size. We will show the effect of equal-cost partitioning as opposed to equal-size partitioning in Section 4.6.2. Unlike radix join, MPSM can partition the private input R completely independent of S. The public input S is partitioned implicitly via the sorting and thus does not incur any partitioning overhead.

4.5 Beyond Inner MPSM and Two-Way Joins

Besides inner join computations, the complex query execution plans evaluated within database systems often contain join variants such as outer joins, semi joins, and anti semi joins. Further, analytical queries often need to join multiple relations and aggregate data in order to provide the information needed. Therefore, in this section, we investigate the effectiveness of MPSM for non-inner join variants and complex query plans composed of multiple operations like joins and aggregations.

4.5 Beyond Inner MPSM and Two-Way Joins

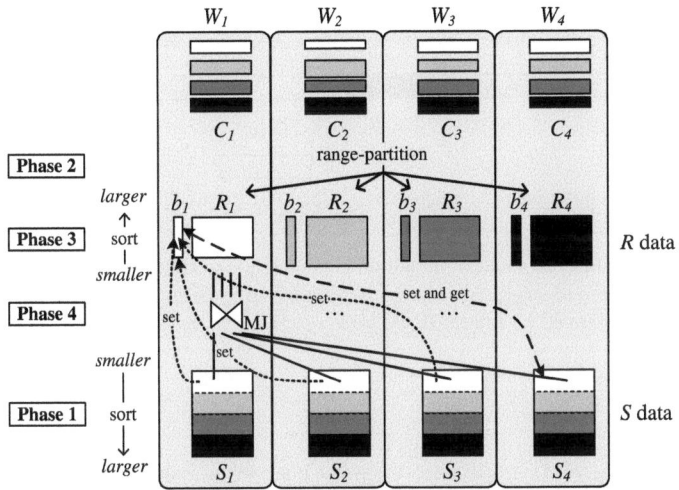

Figure 4.14: Outer and anti semi P-MPSM join with four workers W_i maintaining each an additional joined-bitmap b_i for their private input runs

4.5.1 Outer, Semi, Anti Semi Joins

We first depict the implementation of outer, semi, and anti semi MPSM joins. Depending on whether the private or the public input (or both) produces outer, semi, or anti semi result tuples, additional data structures are required. We will show in Section 4.6.3 that the overhead incurred by these data structures is negligible.

As each thread traverses its private input several times, we need to maintain joined-flags for private input tuples. We then only produce (additional) output tuples if

- no join partner has been found (outer and anti semi join), or if

- the respective tuple has not been joined yet (semi join).

On the contrary, each public input tuple is touched only once due to the implicit partitioning of the public input. Therefore, we can decide right away if outer, semi, or anti semi output tuples have to be produced. Before the join phase 4, outer, semi, and anti semi MPSM join process their inputs the same way as inner MPSM join. If necessary, joined-flags in the form of bitmaps tracking whether private input tuples have (already) been joined are initialized when MPSM enters join phase 4.

While semi joins are very similar to inner joins (output tuples are produced if a join partner has been found), outer and anti semi joins require some attention in order to avoid missing or duplicating output tuples due to range-partitioning and interpolation search. In the following, we briefly describe the implementations of outer, semi, and anti semi MPSM joins. R and S denote the private and the public input, respectively.

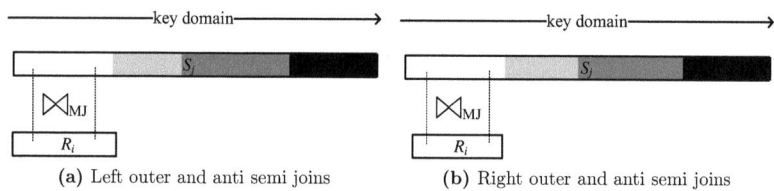

(a) Left outer and anti semi joins   **(b)** Right outer and anti semi joins

Figure 4.15: Outer and anti semi join processing require attention during the join phase: due to interpolation search and early stop of merge join, the red tuples are skipped by inner MPSM join

Outer Joins

Outer joins bring together matching tuples like inner joins, and, in addition, they produce output tuples for input tuples that didn't find a join partner. The left (private input) outer join $R \bowtie S$ requires joined-flags indicating whether the private input tuples already took part in the join or not. Each time a regular join output tuple is generated, the corresponding flag is set. In Figure 4.14, this is indicated by the "set" arrows toward the bitmap, which are shown only for worker W_1 for the sake of readability. During its last, i.e., w^{th}, merge join, in addition to the regular merge join computation, each thread checks the joined-flags and produces output tuples for private input tuples for which the flag is not set. In the example in Figure 4.14, when worker W_1 conducts the last merge join of its private input run R_1 with S_4, it sets flags for joined tuples and gets flags to decide on the generation of additional output tuples ("set and get" arrow from and to bitmap b_1).

As opposed to the computation of inner joins, not only tuples finding a join partner have to be considered but also those that do not find a match. This requires special care: Due to interpolation search, the first private input tuples may be skipped. Further, the last tuples may be skipped as merge join stops early as soon as one of the inputs terminates. These two issues are illustrated in Figure 4.15a where the first and the last tuple of R_i are not considered. In order to not miss outer output tuples, it is therefore crucial for each thread to scan its whole private input (at least) once. Thus, when executing the last (w^{th}) merge join, the threads omit interpolation search on their private input runs and start scanning at the first tuple in their run. This actually mainly affects R_1 as for all other R runs interpolation search is usually performed on S runs. Further, the threads scan their private input run up to its last tuple irrespective of the occurrence of matching tuples in S.

The right (public input) outer join $R \bowtie S$ is straightforward as it can be decided at the time a tuple is processed whether it found a join partner or an extra output tuple has to be returned. However, here again due to interpolation search and early stop of merge join, the first and last tuples of the considered key range may be skipped as illustrated in Figure 4.15b. Therefore, interpolation search on public input runs S_j is not based on tuple key values of R_i but on the splitters determined in phase 2. That way, all S tuples within a worker's key range (white to black shades in the figures) are considered in the join processing.

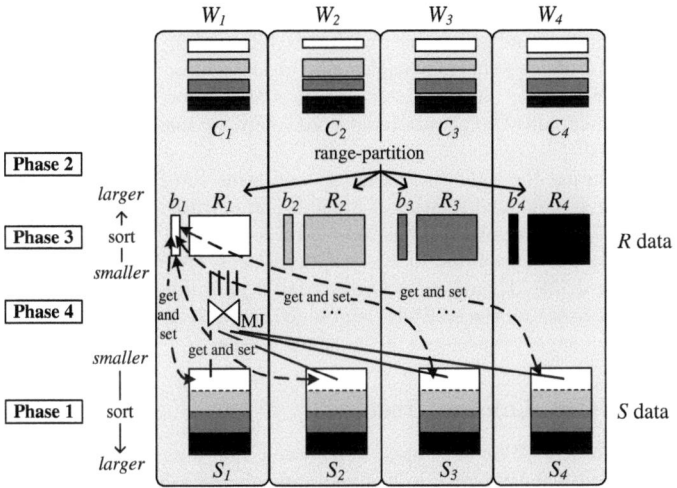

Figure 4.16: Semi P-MPSM join with four workers W_i maintaining each an additional joined-bitmap b_i for their private input runs

Semi Joins

Semi joins produce output for tuples of one of the inputs which find a join partner in the other input. In contrast to inner joins, one input tuple may produce at most one output tuple. For this purpose, the left (private input) semi join $R \ltimes S$ requires joined-flags indicating whether a private input tuple already took part in the join or not. If so, the tuple will not produce any output again. If the flag is not set and a public input tuple matches, an output tuple is produced and the corresponding flag is set. As opposed to left outer joins, the joined-flags are not only checked at the end of the join phase 4 but need to be consulted for each matching tuple during each single merge join. This is illustrated in Figure 4.16 using "get and set" arrows for all merge joins.

For the right (public input) semi join $R \rtimes S$, the private input is scanned for a specific public input tuple until one match is found or the key of the private input is greater than the current public input key. If a match exists, an output tuple is generated and the worker moves on to the next public input tuple as the current may not produce any further output.

Anti Semi Joins

Anti semi joins are the opposite of semi joins. Output is produced for input tuples that do not find a join partner in the other input. The left (private input) anti semi join $R \triangleright S$ requires joined-flags indicating whether the private input tuples already found a join partner or not. Each time a public input tuple matches, the flag for the corresponding private input tuple is set (without producing an output tuple). In Figure 4.14, this is indicated by the "set" arrows toward the joined-bitmap b_1 of worker W_1. As for outer joins, during the last (w^{th}) merge join, in addition to setting flags for joining tuples, each thread checks the bitmap and produces an output tuple for each private input tuple, for which the flag is not set ("set and get" arrow from and to bitmap b_1). Due to interpolation search and early stop of merge join, some tuples may be skipped as illustrated in Figure 4.15a. As for left outer joins, by omitting interpolation search on private input runs for the last merge join and scanning the private input completely, we make sure that no anti output tuples are missed.

When computing the right (public input) anti semi join $R \triangleleft S$, it can be decided at the time a tuple is processed whether it found a join partner or – in case no join partner at all was found – an output tuple has to be returned. Again, we need to make sure that no output tuples are missed due to interpolation search and early stop of merge join as shown in Figure 4.15b. Therefore, as for right outer joins, interpolation search on public input runs S_j is based on the splitters determined in phase 2, so that all S tuples within a worker's key range are considered in the join processing.

4.5.2 The Guy Lohman Test

After having covered MPSM for inner, outer, semi, and anti semi joins, we put MPSM to what Graefe (1993) calls the Guy Lohman test, stating that a join operator must not only be useful for joining two inputs but also in more complex query computations. In particular, an operator is suitable in query processing if it does not require its input(s) to be materialized by preceding operators but allows for pipelining them. MPSM is roughly order preserving, which can be exploited in subsequent join operations of a complex query plan. We depict different ways of how to make use of the output sort order in a sequence of two MPSM joins. Here, we consider the intermediate result to be taken as private or public input for further processing. Teams even go one step further and combine multiple operations in a single one. Thereby, teams are usually more efficient than an equivalent sequential execution of the operations by an effective preprocessing of the data.

We present approaches for the use of MPSM in multiple join operations on the same column(s). They are typical, e.g., for column stores where tables have to be re-established from binary relations. We further discuss their applicability for cases where the joins are executed on different columns.

Initial Situation

Figure 4.17 illustrates the situation after one MPSM join has been executed. Each of the workers produces several sorted output runs covering only a part of the key domain. The intermediate result data is stored locally. A second MPSM join operator may take the intermediate result data as private or as public input depending on its size compared to the third relation to be joined. Assuming certain data distributions (in particular, similar data distributions of the inputs to the first and the second join), we can benefit from the given range-partitioning of the intermediate result. When using it as private input, we can omit re-partitioning the data. When using it as public input, this introduces location skew, i.e., most or all join partners of a private input run will be found in one local or remote public input run. As we will show in Section 4.6.2, this reduces the effective number of merge joins and thus execution time.

Without any knowledge of the data distribution, however, the second MPSM join, which processes the intermediate result and a third relation, is executed as usual. That is, the public input is sorted, the private input is redistributed among the workers and

4.5 Beyond Inner MPSM and Two-Way Joins

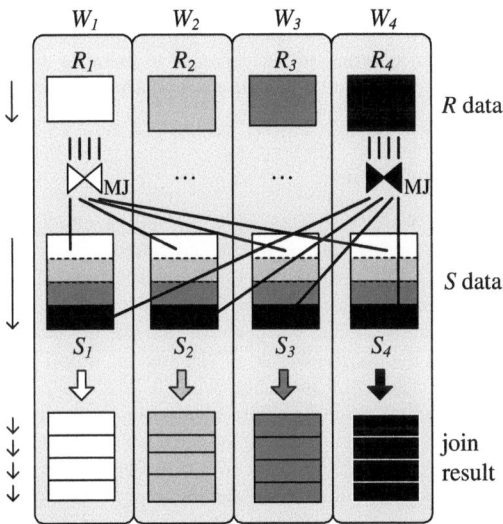

Figure 4.17: Result of P-MPSM join with four workers W_i: each worker produces four sorted (denoted by the arrows on the left) runs covering only its private input run part of the key domain and stores them locally

then sorted, and the private input runs are each merge-joined with all public input runs. We therefore use this scenario as the baseline and compare our approaches presented below to it.

Local Merge of Output Runs

Each worker's output consists of sorted runs within the worker's assigned key range. By merging these output runs, one sorted run of the respective key range is produced. This intermediate result run can then be fed into the second join as private or as public input. Used as private input, we benefit from the given range-partitioning. If there is key value skew within the inputs to the second join, it is handled by computing new splitters and passing consecutive parts of the private input runs to other workers. As the workers' key ranges are disjoint and the data is already sorted, this only requires copying or linking run parts. When used as public input, this introduces location skew, i.e., basically only one merge join pass is required to find all join partners of a private input run as described above.

This variant requires each worker to store its complete intermediate result before it can be merged as the runs are produced subsequently. Furthermore, the sort order within one worker's output runs cannot be exploited if the second join is computed using different join column(s). It is possible, however, to sort the input chunks primarily by the first join column(s) and secondarily by the second during the first join. This requires the second join column(s) to be contained in the respective input relation, which is the case for (at least) one of the inputs. However, this approach incurs high merging overhead (potentially $w \cdot |D|$ runs have to be merged, where D is the value dimension of the first join key). Furthermore, in contrast to the scenario of merging in between joins on the same column(s), the merged output run then contains the complete key range, i.e., it is not range-partitioned.

Concatenation of Output Runs

When concatenating the workers' output runs instead of merging them, each worker obtains one sorted run covering the complete key range. This is achieved by letting each worker W_i collect the ith output run of all workers and append those runs. In contrast to merging, concatenating theoretically does not require the intermediate result to be materialized completely in case we know the size of the intermediate result runs. However, practically this is only applicable in the case of a non-filtered primary key – foreign key join. In other cases, additional buffer might be allocated for the result runs so that they are not completely dense. As the resulting runs cover the complete key range, feeding them into the second join as private input will not be beneficial as no work can be saved. We might only exploit the given sort order to copy whole run parts during scattering instead of considering each tuple on its own. When using the intermediate result runs as public input, sorting can be omitted.

This approach cannot be adapted to work for multiple joins on different columns.

Pipelined Execution

The approaches above share the disadvantage that intermediate results have to be materialized before they can be postprocessed (merged or concatenated) and fed into the second join. This contradicts the Guy Lohman requirements for join operators. We now present a pipelined execution of two subsequent MPSM joins, which exploits the fact that each worker produces sorted output runs and that these runs can immediately be joined with the third relation. In total, each worker then executes quadratic as many merge joins (of smaller inputs) as there are workers (and thus output runs), however, sorting of the third relation and the merge joins between intermediate result runs and runs of the third relation are executed in parallel with the first join processing.

The pipelined MPSM is applicable to joins on different columns. This requires the pipelined intermediate result runs to be sorted by the new join key before they are joined with the third input, thereby probably losing the range-partitioning of the private input. Thus, extra sorting and join overhead is incurred.

MPSM Teams

Teams prepare all inputs to be joined before starting the join phase such that both joins can then be done in one pass. For example, for hash-based join algorithms, this means partitioning all input relations, then loading the corresponding partitions of all relations and producing output tuples as described in Graefe et al. (1998). We adapt this idea to MPSM by preprocessing the relations in the following way: Two of the tables are treated as private inputs, the third table is treated as public input. The private inputs are range-partitioned and sorted according to the join column(s), the public input is sorted by the join column(s). Then, each worker executes multi-way merge joins, reading its private input runs several times and the public input runs only once.

4.5 Beyond Inner MPSM and Two-Way Joins

MPSM teams are not directly applicable for joins on different columns. In case of joins along primary key – foreign key chains with $1 : N$ functionalities, it is, however, possible to map the join keys to new values and allow for team processing even for different join columns. Of course, key-mapping incurs extra overhead. MPSM teams are further easily extensible to compute an aggregation on the join result as part of the team processing. The adaptation of MPSM teams to this scenario is called generalized MPSM teams and adopts the idea of generalized hash teams by Kemper et al. (1999). For a better understanding, we first present a simplified scenario including a join and an aggregation on different columns. The relations are initially partitioned according to the aggregation column(s) in a way that further range-partitions the private and public input by join column(s). In Figure 4.18, we illustrate this for the following query joining the TPC-C benchmark tables Customer and Order on the customer ID and then grouping the join result by the customer's city:

```
SELECT C_City, sum(O_OL_CNT)
FROM Customer, Order
WHERE C_ID = O_C_ID
GROUP BY C_City
```

The Customer relation is first partitioned by C_City. Then, each worker maps the join keys C_ID of its chunk to new C_ID' values, which are assigned to the workers in ascending order and are thus also implicitly range-partitioned. Such a key-mapping is applicable in case the join key is unique. In the example, this is true as the join key C_ID is the primary key of the Customer relation. Thus, the Customer chunks are naturally ordered by C_ID' values and sorting can be omitted. After that, each thread applies the key-mapping to its Order relation chunk and then sorts the chunk by the new O_C_ID' values. Finally, the merge join is executed and (intermediate) aggregation results are computed on the fly. The intermediate results of worker W_i are enhanced with each merge join $R_i \bowtie S_j$, resulting in the final aggregation results after the last (w^{th}) merge join pass.

In the example in Figure 4.18, the Customer relation is not only range-partitioned but also sorted by C_City. This can either be achieved by using histogramming on the aggregation column(s) during partitioning or by explicitly sorting the chunk after range-partitioning. That way, the intermediate aggregation results of a worker W_i can easily be stored and updated together with its private input run data. However, it is also possible to keep the intermediate results in a separate data structure like a hash table, thereby omitting additional histogramming or sort passes on the private input run. In the following, we assume the latter in our cost approximations.

A traditional plan that executes the join and a sort-based aggregation subsequently has the following complexity per worker W_i (denoting Customer as R and Order as S):

$$
\begin{array}{rl}
& |S|/w \cdot log(|S|/w) \quad \text{sort chunk } S_i \text{ of size } |S|/w \\
+ & |R|/w \quad \text{range-partition chunk } R_i \text{ of size } |R|/w \\
+ & |R|/w \cdot log(|R|/w) \quad \text{sort chunk } R_i \text{ of size } |R|/w \\
+ & w \cdot |R|/w \quad \text{process run } R_i \text{ for all } S \text{ runs} \\
+ & w \cdot |S|/w^2 \quad \text{process } 1/w^{\text{th}} \text{ of each } S \text{ run} \\
+ & |J|/w \quad \text{range-partition join result chunk } J_i \text{ of size } |J|/w \\
+ & |J|/w \cdot log(|J|/w) \quad \text{sort join result chunk } J_i \text{ of size } |J|/w \\
+ & |J|/w \quad \text{compute aggregation of join result chunk } J_i \\
\end{array}
$$

$$= |R|/w + |R|/w \cdot log(|R|/w) + |R| + |S|/w + |S|/w \cdot log(|S|/w) + 2 \cdot |J|/w + |J|/w \cdot log(|J|/w)$$

124   4. Massively Parallel Sort-Merge Joins

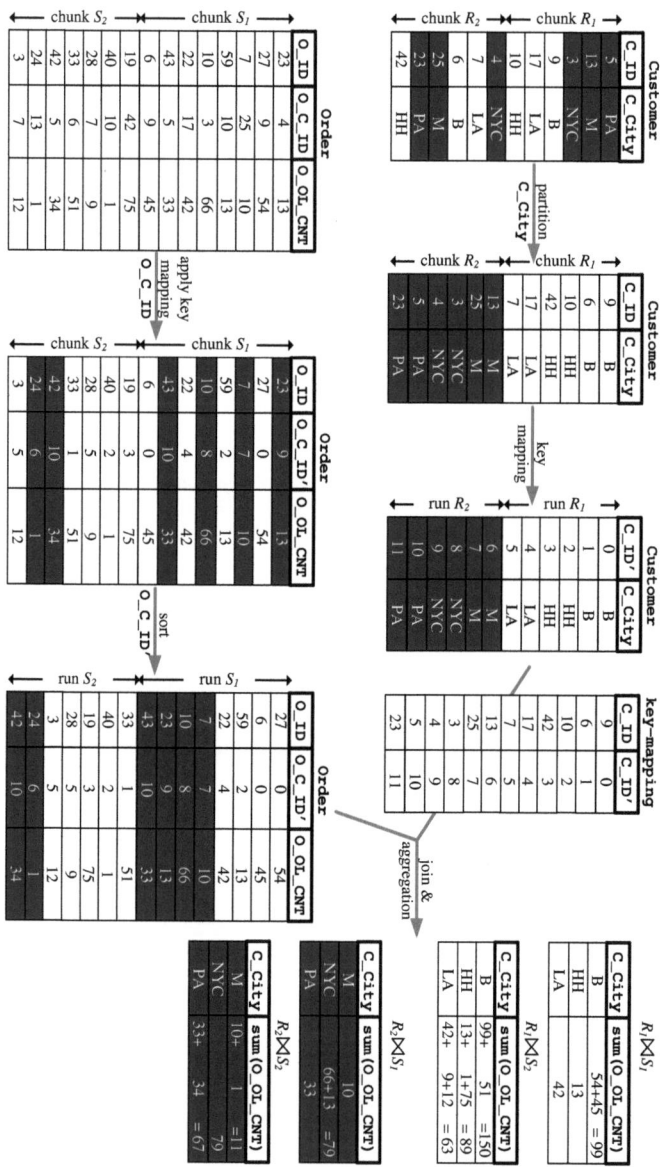

Figure 4.18: Example of MPSM teams for join and aggregation on TPC-C benchmark tables Customer and Order (only relevant columns shown)

In comparison, the generalized MPSM teams execution plan has the following complexity per worker W_i:

	$|R|/w$	range-partition chunk R_i of size $|R|/w$
+	$|R|/w$	create and apply key-mapping to chunk R_i
+	$|S|/w$	apply key-mapping to chunk S_i of size $|S|/w$
+	$|S|/w \cdot log(|S|/w)$	sort chunk S_i of size $|S|/w$
+	$w \cdot |R|/w$	process run R_i for all S runs
+	$w \cdot |S|/w^2$	process $1/w^{\text{th}}$ of each S run

$$= 2 \cdot |R|/w + |R| + 2 \cdot |S|/w + |S|/w \cdot log(|S|/w)$$

Compared to the traditional plan, MPSM teams are preferable with respect to memory requirements and robustness. The traditional plan requires additional space of size $|J|$ to store the intermediate result and additional $2 \cdot |J|/w + |J|/w \cdot log(|J|/w)$ time for the computation of the aggregation result, which depends on the unknown size of J. MPSM teams require only linear additional time $|R|/w + |S|/w$, but can omit sorting the R input chunks. Further, the additional space for the key-mapping can be approximated to be at most $|R|$. The space needed for the intermediate aggregation results is bounded by $|J|$. Thus, in total, MPSM teams eliminate the need for estimating the intermediate result size $|J|$, thereby contributing to robust query processing, and further require less space and computational time.

Due to the required key-mapping, MPSM teams processing is, however, limited to the following scenarios: If the join attribute is a unique key (like C_ID in the example), each worker is assigned a range of ascending and dense C_ID' values for the mapping. After the key-mapping has been applied, the private input chunks are trivially sorted. If the join attribute is not a unique key but it determines the aggregation attribute, i.e., the functional dependency *join attribute* → *aggregation attribute* holds, a certain join attribute value may occur more than once in the input chunks, so that disjoint C_ID' ranges for the workers are determined in a first step based on the number of disjoint key values. After applying the key-mapping to the private input chunks, they need to be sorted. In other cases in which no functional dependencies are given between join attribute and aggregation attribute, the input cannot be partitioned in a way that creates disjoint C_ID' ranges. Therefore, synchronization is required during the key-mapping computation. Further, this case results in inefficient join computations as the input relation is not range-partitioned by the join attribute.

The presented approach is adaptable to allow for multi-way-joins on different columns. The three-way join between the TPC-C tables Customer, Order, and OrderLine with an aggregation on C_City

```
SELECT C_City, sum(OL_Amount)
FROM Customer, Order, OrderLine
WHERE C_ID = O_C_ID
  AND O_ID = OL_O_ID
GROUP BY C_City
```

can be computed in a similar way as illustrated in Figure 4.19. The Customer relation is partitioned according to the aggregation attribute C_City. Then, key-mapping 1 from C_ID to C_ID' is computed and applied to the Customer chunks and the Order chunks. Next, the Order chunks are partitioned and sorted by the new O_C_ID' values. After that, key-mapping 2 from O_ID to O_ID' is computed and applied to the chunks of the Order and OrderLine relations. Finally, the OrderLine chunks are sorted by OL_O_ID' values and the joins are executed in one pass together with the aggregation. For an efficient key-mapping, it is required that the functional dependencies *join attribute 2 → join attribute 1* and *join attribute 1 → aggregation attribute* apply.

A traditional plan that executes the two joins subsequently and then computes the aggregation on the intermediate join result has the following costs per worker W_i (denoting Customer as R, Order as S, and OrderLine as T):

$$
\begin{array}{rl}
& |S|/w \cdot log(|S|/w) \quad \text{sort chunk } S_i \text{ of size } |S|/w \\
+ & |R|/w \quad \text{range-partition chunk } R_i \text{ of size } |R|/w \\
+ & |R|/w \cdot log(|R|/w) \quad \text{sort chunk } R_i \text{ of size } |R|/w \\
+ & w \cdot |R|/w \quad \text{process run } R_i \text{ for all } S \text{ runs} \\
+ & w \cdot |S|/w^2 \quad \text{process } 1/w^{\text{th}} \text{ of each } S \text{ run} \\
+ & |T|/w \cdot log(|T|/w) \quad \text{sort chunk } T_i \text{ of size } |T|/w \\
+ & |J|/w \quad \text{range-partition join 1 result chunk } J_i \text{ of size } |J|/w \\
+ & |J|/w \cdot log(|J|/w) \quad \text{sort join 1 result chunk } J_i \text{ of size } |J|/w \\
+ & w \cdot |J|/w \quad \text{process run } J_i \text{ for all } T \text{ runs} \\
+ & w \cdot |T|/w^2 \quad \text{process } 1/w^{\text{th}} \text{ of each } T \text{ run} \\
+ & |J2|/w \quad \text{range-partition join 2 result chunk } J2_i \text{ of size } |J2|/w \\
+ & |J2|/w \cdot log(|J2|/w) \quad \text{sort join 2 result chunk } J2_i \text{ of size } |J2|/w \\
+ & |J2|/w \quad \text{compute aggregation of join 2 result chunk } J2_i
\end{array}
$$

$= |R|/w + |R|/w \cdot log(|R|/w) + |R| + |S|/w + |S|/w \cdot log(|S|/w) + |T|/w + |T|/w \cdot log(|T|/w) + |J|/w + |J|/w \cdot log(|J|/w) + |J| + 2 \cdot |J2|/w + |J2|/w \cdot log(|J2|/w)$

The generalized MPSM teams plan costs per worker W_i are:

$$
\begin{array}{rl}
& |R|/w \quad \text{range-partition chunk } R_i \text{ of size } |R|/w \\
+ & |R|/w \quad \text{create and apply key-mapping 1 to chunk } R_i \\
+ & |S|/w \quad \text{apply key-mapping 1 to chunk } S_i \text{ of size } |S|/w \\
+ & |S|/w \quad \text{range-partition chunk } S_i \text{ of size } |S|/w \\
+ & |S|/w \cdot log(|S|/w) \quad \text{sort chunk } S_i \text{ of size } |S|/w \\
+ & |S|/w \quad \text{create and apply key-mapping 2 to chunk } S_i \\
+ & |T|/w \quad \text{apply key-mapping 2 to chunk } T_i \text{ of size } |T|/w \\
+ & |T|/w \cdot log(|T|/w) \quad \text{sort chunk } T_i \text{ of size } |T|/w \\
+ & w \cdot |R|/w \quad \text{process run } R_i \text{ for each } S_i \text{ and all } T \text{ runs} \\
+ & w \cdot |S|/w \quad \text{process run } S_i \text{ for each } R_i \text{ and all } T \text{ runs} \\
+ & w \cdot |T|/w^2 \quad \text{process } 1/w^{\text{th}} \text{ of each } T \text{ run for all pairs of runs } (R_i, S_i)
\end{array}
$$

$= 2 \cdot |R|/w + |R| + 3 \cdot |S|/w + |S|/w \cdot log(|S|/w) + |S| + 2 \cdot |T|/w + |T|/w \cdot log(|T|/w)$

Again, the total costs of the traditional execution plan depend heavily on the size of the intermediate results. They may be misestimated by the optimizer, causing performance degradations. On the other hand, all input sizes of the generalized MPSM teams plan are known. Thus, generalized MPSM teams are preferable from a robustness perspective. Further, the traditional plan incurs additional space requirements of $|J|$ to materialize the intermediate join result. MPSM teams only require little additional space for the intermediate aggregation results.

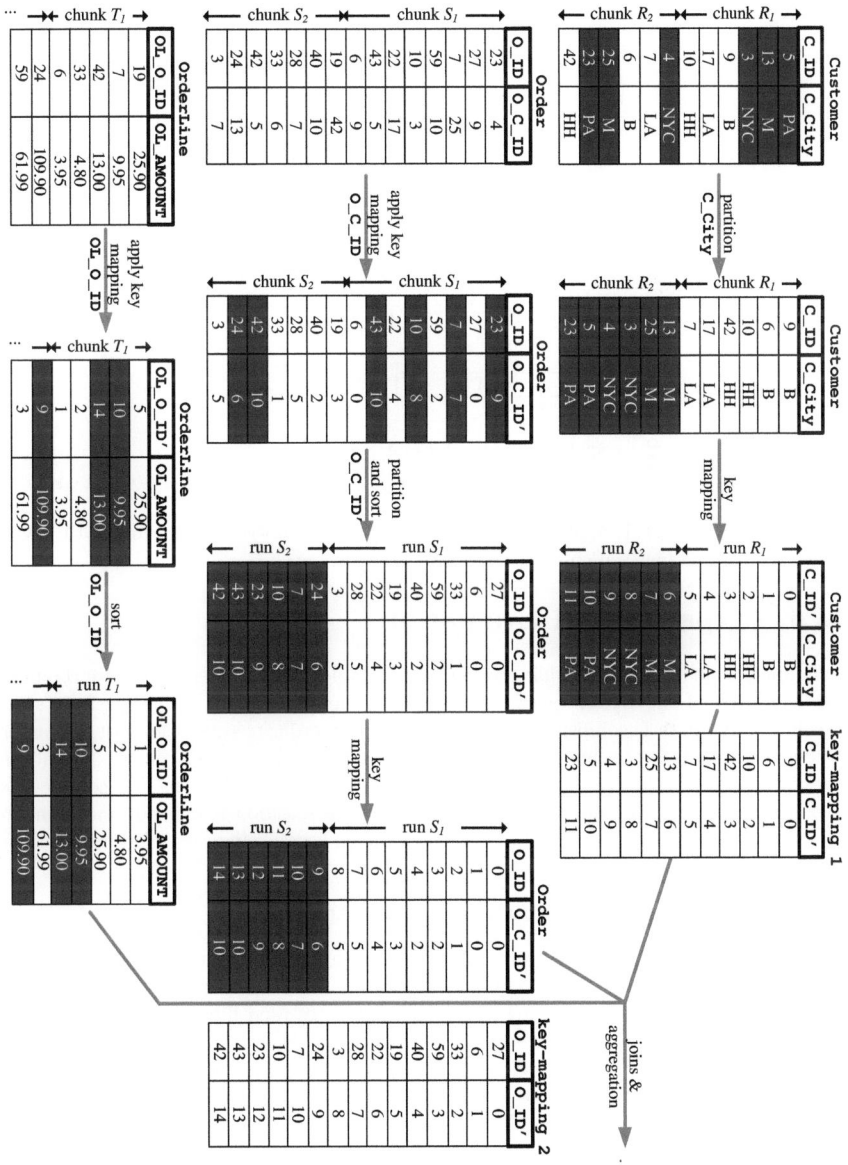

Figure 4.19: Example of MPSM teams for multi-way join and aggregation on TPC-C benchmark tables Customer, Order, and OrderLine (only relevant columns shown)

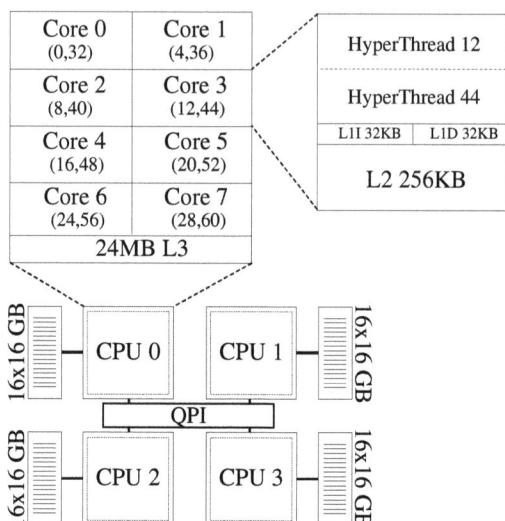

Figure 4.20: HyPer1: Linux server with 1 TB main memory and four Intel CPUs with 8 physical cores (16 hardware contexts) each

4.6 Experimental Evaluation

We implemented the MPSM join variants in C++, and the join query plans are compiled as employed in the HyPer query processor by Neumann (2011). All experiments are such that the data is completely in main memory. In order to cover the most important scenarios, we report benchmark results using datasets which represent join input relations of different sizes, different multiplicities, and different data distributions. We consider the common case that the input relations are scanned, a selection is applied, and then the results are joined. So, no referential integrity (foreign keys) or indexes could be exploited.

4.6.1 Platform and Benchmark Scenarios

We conducted the experiments on a Linux server (kernel 3.0.0) with 1 TB main memory and four Intel(R) Xeon(R) X7560 CPUs clocked at 2.27 GHz with 8 physical cores (16 hardware contexts) each, resulting in a total of 32 cores (and due to hyperthreading 64 hardware contexts). The architecture of the server, which is called HyPer1 in our lab, is depicted in Figure 4.20. This machine currently has a list price of approximately €40 000, which makes it a good candidate for the real-time business intelligence (BI) scenario on transactional data, for which the HyPer main memory database system is intended.

We chose the datasets to be representative for a few realistic data warehouse scenarios. Each dataset for the experiments on a single join operator consists of two relations R and S. The cardinality of R is $1600M$[17], the cardinality of S is scaled to be $1 \cdot |R|$, $4 \cdot |R|$, $8 \cdot |R|$, and $16 \cdot |R|$. Our datasets of cardinality $1600M \cdot (1+\text{multiplicity})$ have sizes ranging from

---

[17]$M = 2^{20}$

4.6 Experimental Evaluation

multiplicity	R		S	
	cardinality	size [GB]	cardinality	size [GB]
1	$1600M$	25	$1600M$	25
4	$1600M$	25	$6400M$	100
8	$1600M$	25	$12800M$	200
16	$1600M$	25	$25600M$	400

Table 4.1: Multiplicities and resulting data sizes for the experiments[17]

50 GB to 425 GB, which is representative for large main memory operational BI workloads. The multiplicities between the relations R and S further cover a wide range, including not only the common cases (4 as specified for instance in TPC-H and 8 to approximate the TPC-C specification) but also extreme cases (1 and 16). These database sizes are one order of magnitude larger than in prior related studies by Kim et al. (2009), Blanas et al. (2011), and Blanas and Patel (2011) to account for recent hardware improvements in RAM capacity and real-world requirements in operational business intelligence. For example, Amazon has a yearly revenue of $40 billion, for which an estimated item price of $10 results in 4 billion orderline tuples – a size which is covered by our experiments. It is interesting to note that the transactional sales data of this largest merchandiser, if properly normalized and possibly compressed, fits into the RAM of our 1 TB machine. This makes operational BI on main-memory-resident data a reality – if the parallelization power of these machines can be effectively exploited.

The multiplicities and relation sizes of our datasets are summarized in Table 4.1. For the experiments on multi-way joins, we extended the datasets by a third relation, which is scaled in the same way.

Each tuple consists of a 64-bit key within the domain $[0, 2^{32})$ and a 64-bit payload:

$$\{[joinkey: \text{uint64\_t}, payload: \text{uint64\_t}]\}$$

We chose the data format both for scaling reasons (payload may represent a record ID or a data pointer) as well as for ease of comparison to the experiments presented in Blanas et al. (2011). If not stated otherwise, the experiments are conducted using a parallelism of 32 (equal to the number of physical cores) and the key values are uniformly distributed resulting in a join selectivity of approximately 0.02% for the tested multiplicities.

4.6.2 Evaluation of MPSM for Inner Joins

To evaluate the performance of MPSM for inner joins, we execute the following equi-join on two tables R and S:

```
SELECT max(R.payload + S.payload)
FROM R, S
WHERE R.joinkey = S.joinkey
```

This query is designed to ensure that the payload data is fed through the join while only one output tuple is generated in order to concentrate on join processing cost only. Further, we made sure that early aggregation was not used by any system.

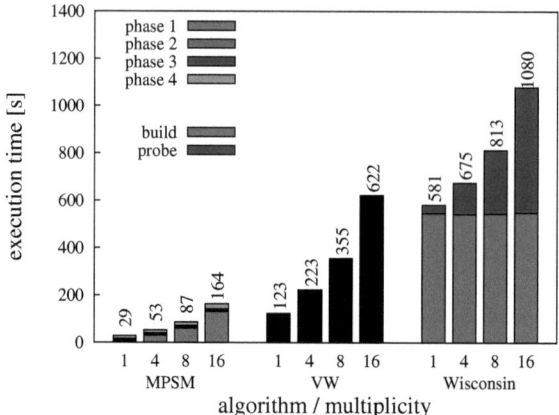

Figure 4.21: Performance comparison of MPSM, Vectorwise (VW), and Wisconsin hash join on uniform data

As "contenders" we chose the most recent research system published by the Wisconsin database group in Blanas et al. (2011) and the "cutting-edge" Vectorwise query engine, which holds the world record in single-server TPC-H power test. According to our tests, it currently has the best-performing parallel join processing engine which is based on the pioneering MonetDB work on cache-friendly radix joins by Manegold et al. (2002). This is also testified by Vectorwise's record TPC-H powertest performance on "small" main-memory-fitting databases up to 1 TB on a single machine. Actually, the TPC-H record numbers were obtained on a similar machine as HyPer1. For the Wisconsin hash join benchmarks, we use the original code of Blanas et al. (2011). The Vectorwise benchmarks are conducted on Vectorwise Enterprise Edition 2.0. In order to obtain benchmark results on main-memory-resident data for the disk-enabled Vectorwise, we execute the query several times and report only the execution times of runs after the data is fully resident in RAM.

Comparison of MPSM, Vectorwise, and Wisconsin join on uniform data

We first compare the performance of MPSM, Vectorwise, and Wisconsin join on uniform data for different multiplicities ranging from 1 to 16, i.e., in the extreme case, S is 16 times as large as R. The results are shown in Figure 4.21. MPSM outperforms Vectorwise by a factor of four for all tested multiplicities. Further, MPSM outperforms the Wisconsin hash join by a factor of up to 17. The poor performance of the Wisconsin hash join in our experiment is due to the fact that it is not adapted to efficiently work for NUMA architectures as it builds and probes a global hash table across NUMA partitions. Therefore, we don't consider it in further experiments.

Scalability in the number of cores

Next, we investigate the ability of MPSM and Vectorwise to exploit highly parallel multi-core architectures. Therefore, we compare their scalability with respect to the number of

4.6 Experimental Evaluation

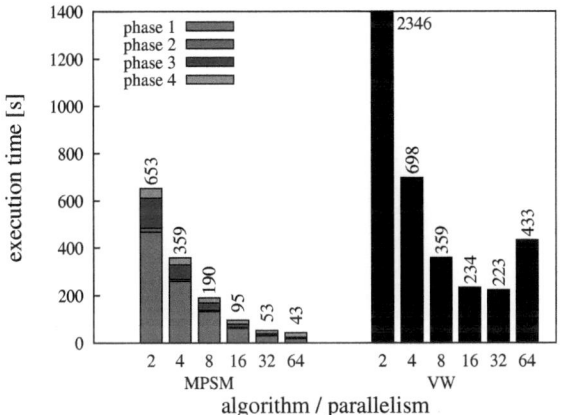

Figure 4.22: Scalability of MPSM and Vectorwise

cores and report the results in Figure 4.22. The multiplicity is fixed to 4 in this experiment. MPSM scales almost linearly in the number of parallel worker threads, i.e., the execution time halves when we double the parallelism level. As depicted in Figure 4.20, our server has 32 physical cores and a total of 64 hardware contexts. When exceeding the number of physical cores and using hyperthreading (parallelism level 64), the performance of MPSM improves only slightly as all cores are already almost fully utilized at parallelism 32. Vectorwise achieves (almost) linear scalability in the number of cores only up to parallelism level 16. When using hyperthreading, the performance even degrades. From these results, we are confident that – contrary to Vectorwise – MPSM will scale well on future hardware with even hundreds of cores.

Role reversal

We mentioned in Section 4.2.3 that it is advisable for P-MPSM to consider role reversal for performance improvements. In Figure 4.23, we compare the execution time for two relations R and S where we vary the size of S to be *multiplicity* times the size of R. As we switch the roles of R and S, phase 1 (sorting the public input) and phase 3 (sorting the private input) are interchanged and have the same execution time when summed up. However, the effect of role reversal is clearly visible for the range-partitioning phase 2 and the join phase 4. For multiplicity 1, role reversal obviously has no effect on the join execution time (as both inputs have the same size). However, the larger S grows, the more considerable is the effect that directly follows from the complexity estimate in Section 4.2.3:

$$\underbrace{|R|/w + |R|/w \cdot log(|R|/w) + |R| + |S|/w + |S|/w \cdot log(|S|/w)}_{R \text{ is private input}}$$

vs.

$$\underbrace{|S|/w + |S|/w \cdot log(|S|/w) + |S| + |R|/w + |R|/w \cdot log(|R|/w)}_{S \text{ is private input}}$$

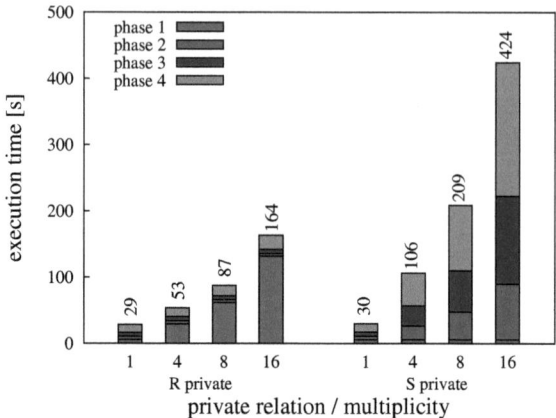

Figure 4.23: Effect of role reversal on join execution time

When ignoring the equal sort costs, this results in:

$$\underbrace{|R|/w + |R| + |S|/w}_{R \text{ is private input}} \text{ vs. } \underbrace{|S|/w + |S| + |R|/w}_{S \text{ is private input}}$$

As it holds that $|R| \leq |S|$, taking R as private input results in the better performance.

Location skew

In order to investigate the effect of location skew on the performance of MPSM, we introduced extreme location skew by arranging S in small to large join key order in a way that all join partners of one private input run R_i are found in only one public input run S_j. It is important to note that this did not introduce a total order of S keys, so sorting the clusters was still necessary. Location skew on R has no effect at all as R is redistributed anyway. The extreme location skew in S results in each worker W_i effectively producing join results only with one local S_i, respectively one remote S_j where $i \neq j$. That is, either only local S data or no local S data at all contribute to the join result and only one remote memory area has to be accessed. Of course, all runs are still accessed using interpolation search, however, no relevant data is found in $(w-1)$ of the S runs. This effectively reduces the complexity from

$$|S|/w \cdot log(|S|/w) + |R|/w + |R|/w \cdot log(|R|/w) + |\mathbf{R}| + |S|/w$$

to

$$|S|/w \cdot log(|S|/w) + |R|/w + |R|/w \cdot log(|R|/w) + |\mathbf{R}|/\mathbf{w} + |S|/w$$

as the private input run R_i is only scanned once to produce all join results. If there is less pronounced location skew in S, the algorithm performance lies between those two extremes shown in Figure 4.24. Note that, in all other experiments, location skew was not present, i.e., the effects of location skew showed in this experiment were not exploited.

4.6 Experimental Evaluation

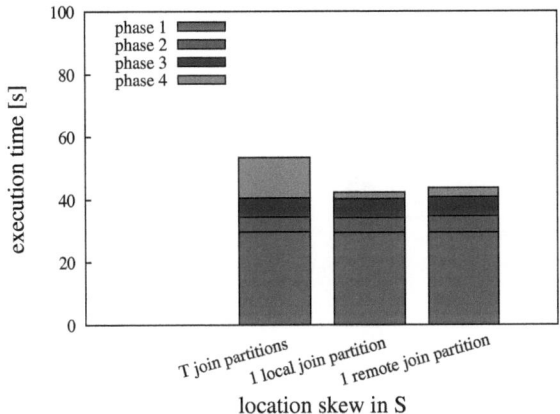

Figure 4.24: Effect of location skew on MPSM performance (multiplicity 4)

Skewed data with negative correlation

In this experiment, we analyze the quality of the splitter computation discussed in Section 4.4 to balance the load evenly across all workers. For this purpose, we generated a dataset with the worst possible skew for our join algorithm: negatively correlated skew in R and S. (Positively correlated skew does not affect MPSM either due to the dynamic splitter computation.) Our data set again contained $1600M$ tuples in R with an 80:20 distribution of the join keys: 80% of the join keys were generated at the 20% *high* end of the domain. The S data of cardinality $4 \cdot 1600M$ was generated with opposite skew: 80% of the join keys were within the 20% *low* end of the domain.

Let us refer to Figure 4.25a to intuitively explain the necessity of balancing the load according to the data distribution of R **and** S. On the left-hand side, we show the effects of partitioning R into equal-cardinality partitions, thereby having wider key ranges on the left and narrower ranges on the right. Because of the negative correlation, the corresponding S partitions are very unbalanced. So, the combined cardinality of the two partitions $|R_i| + |S_{R_i}|$ is much higher at the low end than at the high end. S_{R_i} denotes the relevant join range of S for the key range of R_i. Note that S_{R_i} is composed of subpartitions across all $S_1, \cdots, S_w$, but its size can effectively be estimated from the CDF. For 32 workers operating on this equi-height R partitioning, we obtain the response times shown in Figure 4.25b. We see that the "blue" sort costs are balanced but the "green" join processing takes much longer for the workers on the left that process the low join keys. The correct splitter-based partitioning balances the load across all servers as shown in Figure 4.25c. This is achieved by considering the cardinality of each R_i in combination with its corresponding S_{R_i} partition, which is obtained from the CDF. The balanced R-and-S partitioning is visualized in Figure 4.25a on the right-hand side. The figure is idealized in balancing the cardinality of the two corresponding partitions. In reality, the sort+join **costs** are balanced. For this experiment, we computed the R histograms at a granularity of 1024 ($B = 10$) to give the splitter computation sufficient opportunity to find best possible balanced splitters.

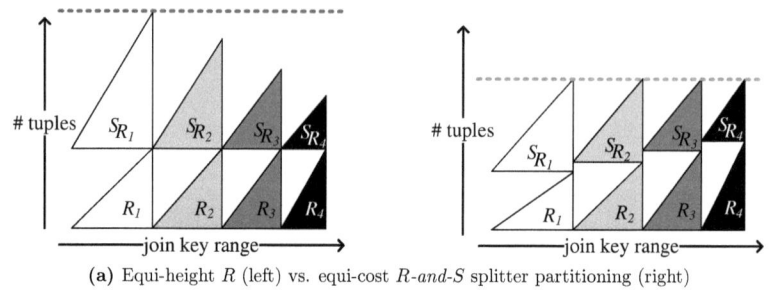

(a) Equi-height R (left) vs. equi-cost R-and-S splitter partitioning (right)

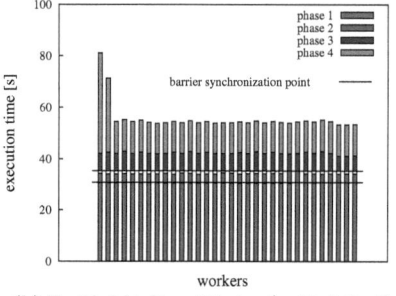

(b) Equi-height R partitioning (multiplicity 4)

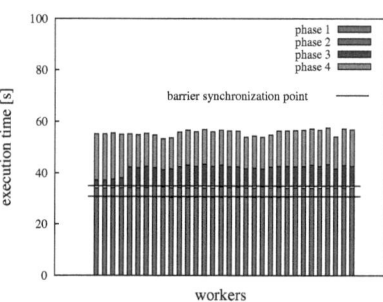

(c) Equi-cost R-and-S splitter partitioning (multiplicity 4)

Figure 4.25: Effect of balancing splitters on MPSM performance

4.6.3 Performance Comparison of Inner, Outer, Semi, and Anti Semi MPSM Joins

To evaluate the performance of MPSM for non-inner joins, we execute the following equi-join on two tables R and S:

```
SELECT count(*)
FROM R <join variant> S
WHERE R.joinkey = S.joinkey
```

The term `<join variant>` stands for left outer join, right outer join, left semi join, right semi join, left anti semi join, and right anti semi join, respectively.

In Figure 4.26, we compare the execution times of the inner MPSM join as evaluated in Section 4.6.2 and the non-inner join variants for multiplicities between 1 and 16. The numbers of inner, semi, and outer result tuples for the tested datasets are listed in Table 4.2. The larger the S relation, the larger is the number of inner, left semi, and right semi result tuples as the key values are uniformly distributed within the domain. The number of left outer and left anti result tuples decreases with increasing multiplicity, as more tuples find a join partner. On the contrary, the number of right outer and right anti result tuples increases with increasing multiplicity, as the potential join partners in the left relation remain the same.

4.6 Experimental Evaluation

Multiplicity	Approximate number of result tuples						
	I	LO	RO	LS	RS	LA	RA
1	$625M$	$1083M$	$1083M$	$517M$	$517M$	$1083M$	$1083M$
4	$2500M$	$335M$	$4330M$	$1265M$	$2070M$	$335M$	$4330M$
8	$5000M$	$70M$	$8661M$	$1530M$	$4139M$	$70M$	$8661M$
16	$10000M$	$3M$	$17322M$	$1597M$	$8278M$	$3M$	$17322M$

Table 4.2: Number of inner (I), pure left outer (LO), pure right outer (RO), left semi (LS), right semi (RS), left anti semi (LA), and right anti semi (RA) result tuples for the tested datasets

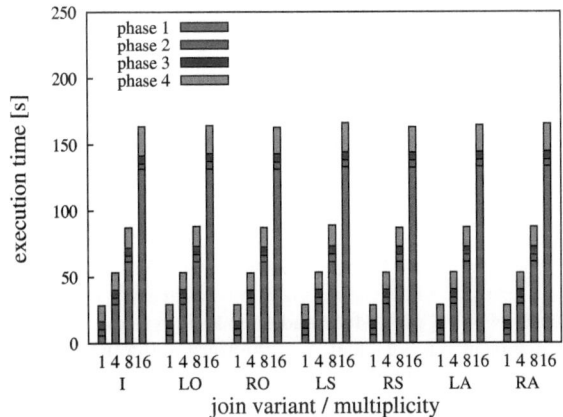

Figure 4.26: Performance comparison of inner (I), left outer (LO), right outer (RO), left semi (LS), right semi (RS), left anti semi (LA), and right anti semi (RA) MPSM join

The non-inner join variants described in Section 4.5 incur no (in case of right outer, semi, and anti semi joins) or only little overhead for tracking whether one tuple of the left input already found a join partner in the right input (in case of left outer, semi, and anti semi joins). The modification of the interpolation search required for outer and anti semi joins does not incur additional overhead. In total, we find that the performance decrease caused by the additional data structures is negligible.

4.6.4 Exploiting MPSM Characteristics in Complex Query Plans

We examine the suitability of MPSM for complex query plans on the example of a three way equi-join between the tables R, S, and T on the same join key:

```
SELECT max(R.payload + S.payload + T.payload)
FROM R, S, T
WHERE R.joinkey = S.joinkey
  AND S.joinkey = T.joinkey
```

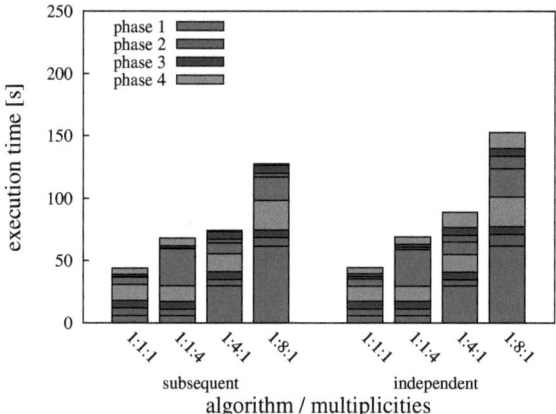

Figure 4.27: Performance comparison of two subsequent MPSM join executions and two independent MPSM joins

We compare the alternatives of exploiting the rough sort order of the MPSM output presented in Section 4.5.2 to the baseline case where two MPSM joins are executed subsequently without postprocessing the intermediate result. We report experiments using the multiplicities $1:1:1$, $1:1:4$, $1:4:1$, and $1:8:1$. In a perfect scenario, an optimizer would always join smaller relations first, i.e., the third and fourth case would not occur. However, we included those experiments to cover cases in which the intermediate result is smaller than the third table and cases in which it is larger, without modifying the key ranges or uniformity of the data distribution. In our experiments, for multiplicity $1:1:1$, the intermediate result is a little smaller than the third relation, for $1:1:4$ it is much smaller, for $1:4:1$ it is a little larger, and for $1:8:1$ it is much larger.

Implicit Benefits of Subsequent MPSM Joins

We first want to point out that two subsequent MPSM joins in one query plan implicitly benefit from locality of the data and range-partitioning. As illustrated in Figure 4.17, each worker's output runs are stored locally and cover only part of the key domain. A second operator (not changing the affinity of threads to cores) can therefore initially work on local data and, in case of a second MPSM, it profits from the location skew introduced by the first operator. In Figure 4.27, we compare the execution times of two independent MPSM joins and two subsequent MPSM joins. The positive effect shows in different phases, depending on whether the intermediate result is taken as private input (cases $1:1:1$ and $1:1:4$) or as public input (cases $1:4:1$ and $1:8:1$). In the two leftmost bars, the effect is visible in the second join's phase 2 (upper red) and phase 3 (upper blue) execution times. In the two rightmost bars, it is visible in the second join's phase 1 (upper gray) and phase 4 (upper green) execution times. In total, the execution time benefits of two subsequent MPSM joins compared to two independent MPSM joins account for up to 20%.

4.6 Experimental Evaluation

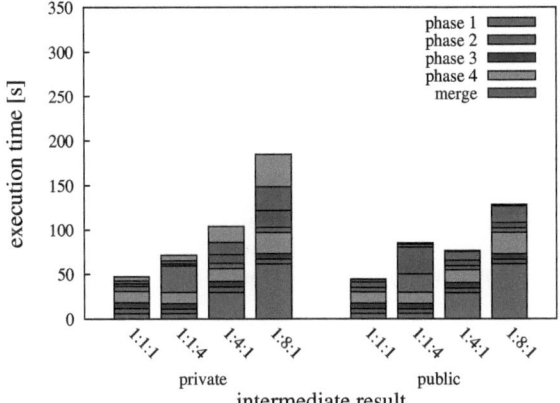

(a) Merging the intermediate result runs between two subsequent MPSM joins

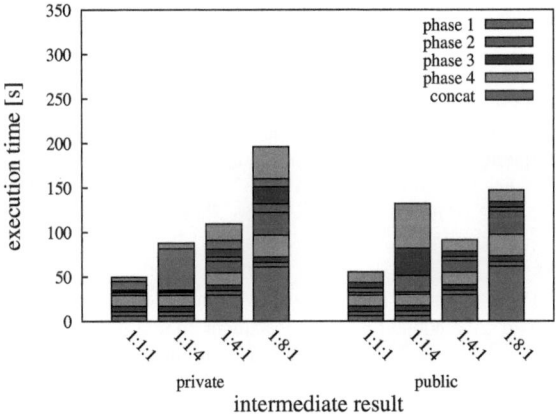

(b) Concatenating the intermediate result runs between two subsequent MPSM joins

Figure 4.28: Two subsequent MPSM joins exploiting the rough sort order of the intermediate result runs

Merge and Concatenation of Intermediate Result Runs

When executing two subsequent MPSM joins, we can postprocess the roughly sorted output of the first join so that the second join profits. In Section 4.5.2, we presented two variants of postprocessing the intermediate result: merge and concatenation of the workers' output runs. In Figure 4.28, we present the resulting performance when we apply these techniques to the intermediate result runs and then feed the result into the second join, once as private input and once as public input. We find that, as we theoretically analyzed in Section 4.2.3 and showed for a single MPSM join computation in Section 4.6.2, the smaller relation should always be picked as the private input. In the following, we therefore assume the optimizer to correctly assign private and public input roles to the smaller, respectively larger relations after the first join.

Comparison to Baseline

In Figure 4.29, we compare the total execution time of two MPSM joins using the approaches described in Section 4.5.2 to that of two subsequent MPSM executions without any additional processing of the intermediate result, which represents the baseline. Overall, the simple execution of two MPSM joins shows the best performance.

Merge. Merging the intermediate result runs to use them as private input to the second join allows for omitting the sort phase in case of uniform key value distribution as given in this experiment. However, merging shows approximately the same performance as the optimized sorting technique of MPSM combining radix and insertion sort. When the merged runs are used as public input, this has the same positive effect as location skew. Two subsequent MPSM joins benefit from location skew as well (see Figure 4.27) and thus result in the same performance.

Concat. Concatenating the result runs is less beneficial when using the outcome as private input to the second join. This is because those runs cover the complete key range and thus must be range-partitioned as usual, resulting in a performance comparable to that of two subsequent MPSM joins. When using the intermediate result runs as public input, the performance is even below that of the baseline because concatenating the runs from multiple remote NUMA partitions is slower than sorting the own runs within the local partition.

Teams. The MPSM teams are not competitive at all as three-way merge-joining incurs a very high overhead. We conclude that subsequent merge joins are more efficient than three-way merge-joins and propose to investigate a team processing variant in which the join phase is adapted to this finding.

Pipelined MPSM

For the evaluation of pipelined MPSM, we instantiate 16 workers to process the first join and another 16 workers to which the intermediate results are piped. The total number of worker threads thus equals the number of physical cores on our server.

Figure 4.30 shows the comparison of two subsequent MPSM joins to pipelined MPSM. Here, "rest" denotes the time from the completion of the first join until the second join execution finishes. Due to the additional bandwidth incurred by the parallel processing of the first join and operations (sorting of the third relation and merge-joining) of the second join, the performance of the first join degrades slightly. Overall, there is no significant performance difference between the two three-way join variants tested in this experiment.

4.6 Experimental Evaluation

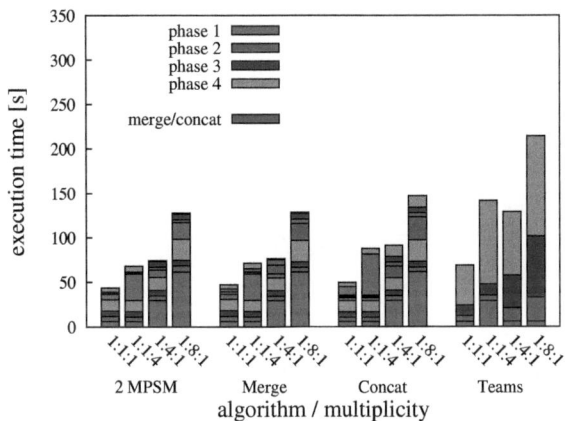

Figure 4.29: Performance comparison of two subsequent MPSM joins without postprocessing the intermediate result (2 MPSM), with merging each worker's intermediate result runs (Merge), and with concatenating the intermediate result runs (Concat)

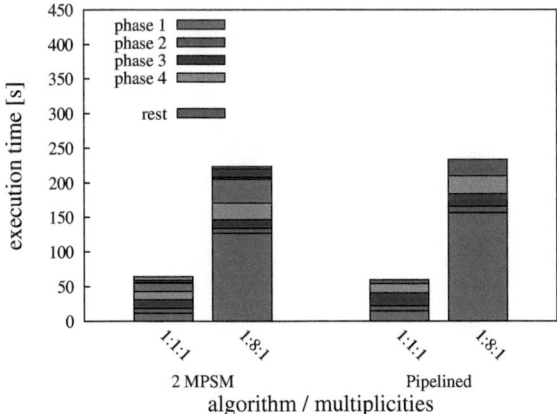

Figure 4.30: Performance comparison of two subsequent MPSM joins without postprocessing the intermediate result (2 MPSM) and pipelined MPSM (16 workers)

4.7 Related Work

Parallel join processing originates from early work on database machines, e.g., Gamma by DeWitt et al. (1992), where hash-based partitioning was used to distribute the join argument to multiple machines in a compute cluster. In this context, some heuristics for skew handling were developed by DeWitt et al. (1990). Frey et al. (2009) and Teubner and Müller (2011) presented parallel joins for modern distributed databases. In multi-core parallel processing, the distribution of the data is much more efficient as we can exploit the shared memory, albeit regarding the consequences of the NUMA architecture as pointed out by Ott (2009). Our MPSM join is, to the best of our knowledge, the first work that consequently takes NUMA into consideration, which is decisive for large-scale in-core databases. Most previous approaches to in-core parallel join processing were based on the radix join pioneered by the MonetDB group, in particular by Manegold et al. (2002) and Boncz et al. (1999). This join method achieves cache locality by continuously partitioning into ever smaller chunks that ultimately fit into the cache. Chen et al. (2007) improved cache locality during the probing phase of the hash join using software controlled prefetching. Our sort-based MPSM algorithm has high cache locality and hardware prefetcher affinity by its very own merge join behavior that sequentially scans a pair of runs.

Kim et al. (2009) adapted hash join to modern multi-core CPUs in an Intel / Oracle cooperation. They also investigated sort-merge join and hypothesized that, due to architectural trends of wider SIMD, more cores, and smaller memory bandwidth per core, sort-merge join is likely to outperform hash join on upcoming chip multiprocessors. Blanas et al. (2011) and Blanas and Patel (2011) presented even better performance results for their parallel hash join variants. We compare the sort-based MPSM to their best-performing variant, which we called Wisconsin hash join here, and thereby pick the competition between sort-merge join and hash join up once again as done by Graefe (1994). As a second contender, we chose Vectorwise Inkster et al. (2011) that builds on the pioneering radix join work of MonetDB published by Boncz et al. (2009) in addition to vector-based processing of X100.

He et al. (2008) developed parallel nested-loops, sort-merge, and hash joins on GPUs. The algorithms take advantage of massive thread parallelism, fast inter-processor communication through local memory, and histograms-based radix-partitioning. We adapted the histogram approach for synchronization-free partitioning of MPSM's private input. For sorting in MPSM, we developed our own combined radix / insertion sort. In the future, however, wider SIMD registers will allow to explore bitonic SIMD sorting as shown by Chhugani et al. (2008).

MPSM does not produce completely sorted output. However, each worker's partition is subdivided into sorted runs. This interesting physical property might be exploited in further operations as shown in Claußen et al. (2000). Note that the algorithms we compared MPSM against do not exhibit any interesting physical property in their output data and we did **not** exploit any possibly pre-existing sorting in our comparative performance experiments.

Our disk-based D-MPSM was partly inspired by g-join by Graefe (2012), which also operates on sorted runs instead of hash partitions as introduced in Graefe (1994). However, g-join lacks the parallelism, which is in the focus of this work.

4.8 Summary and Conclusions

Currently, the two dominating hardware trends are increasing RAM sizes of up to several TB and ever more (soon hundreds of) cores per server. Both facilitate the development of main memory databases that are essential to propel operational/real-time business intelligence (BI) applications, which are gaining more and more importance for the day-to-day business of companies.

In this context, we devised a massively parallel algorithm for the most important query processing operator, the equi-join. It effectively exploits the parallelization potential of today's hardware in order to minimize query response times. MPSM merge-joins sorted runs in parallel, which themselves were sorted by parallel threads. The performance analysis revealed that MPSM can effectively join very large main memory data consisting of billions of tuples as it scales almost linearly with the number of cores. MPSM achieves a join performance of up to 175 million tuples per second (Figure 4.21). Thereby, it outperforms Vectorwise by a factor of four and the Wisconsin hash join by a factor of up to 17. Further, MPSM performs better than the algorithm presented by Kim et al. (2009), which achieved 100-128 million tuples per second on smaller datasets (by more than an order of magnitude) using smaller tuples (i.e., half-sized tuples of 32-bit key and 32-bit payload).

The scalable performance of MPSM is due to carefully exploiting the NUMA characteristics of modern high-capacity servers. We avoided fine-grained synchronization and random accesses to remote NUMA memory partitions. The linear scalability in the number of cores (Figure 4.22) promises the MPSM join to scale even beyond our tested 32 core, 1 TB server, which is currently the top of the line main memory server but will soon be surpassed by the next generations of servers.

Even though MPSM exploits radix-partitioning to minimize the merge join costs, it is robust with respect to skew by determining the partition bounds dynamically using efficiently computed approximations of the input data distributions and applying the splitter computation adapted from Ross and Cieslewicz (2009). We demonstrated this for the worst possible scenario for MPSM, which is negatively correlated skew (Figure 4.25).

Further, we developed the algorithmic details of MPSM for join variants other than inner join, i.e., outer, semi, and anti semi joins. They require only slight modifications to the inner join algorithm and the overhead caused by the additional data structures and computations is negligible (Figure 4.15). We also worked on exploiting the rough sort order that MPSM inherently generates due to its range-partitioned merge join processing. We compared the effect of merging and concatenating intermediate result runs to that of MPSM teams, which process a three-way join in one operation (Figure 4.29). Furthermore, we investigated a pipelined version of MPSM (Figure 4.30). The experimental evaluation revealed that the efficient sort and merge join phases of MPSM leave almost no room for improvement.

Lastly, MPSM is adaptable to I/O-bound scenarios, in which intermediate results are written to disk. The disk-enabled D-MPSM is particularly promising for large batch query processing tasks that take place in parallel with transactions and real-time BI analytics.

Chapter 5

Summary and Conclusions

Scalable analytical query processing gained renewed interest as the growing demand for real-time business intelligence led to the reintegration of OLTP and OLAP processing within one database system. The challenge here is to efficiently execute analytical workloads in order to provide useful information for strategic planning within short response times while impacting the performance of time-critical transactional workloads, which are crucial for the day-to-day business, as little as possible.

In this work, we developed approaches for the efficient, robust, and scalable execution of OLAP workloads. We first considered the workloads as a whole and exploited the interactions of concurrently executing queries within a workload. We found that they might influence each other either positively or negatively. The synergy between two queries depends on a multitude of factors, e.g., the system's hardware and configuration, implementation details of the database operators, and programs running on the same system as the database. The effects of these sources of synergies overlap and may cancel each other out. Thus, the prediction of query influences is a complex task and prediction models are often based on probably arguable assumptions. We therefore pursued a different approach considering the database as a black box and assuming we have no prior knowledge about the workload. In our approach, we relied on the fact that both positive and negative synergies between queries are reflected by the execution time of these queries. By monitoring the execution times of different query sets at runtime, we drew conclusions regarding the synergies of queries. For this purpose, we defined a system of equations containing all available information about query set execution times and solved it by uniformly distributing uncertainty over the variables. An optimization component between client and database system transparently monitors execution times and feeds them into synergy computation. Depending on the database load, it adaptively switches between training and optimization. We analyzed different scheduling approaches for the training and the optimization phases. During the training, the main goal of scheduling is acquiring maximal knowledge of synergies between the workload's queries. We showed that we can obtain useful information about synergies within short time. Scheduling algorithms that quickly fill the synergy matrix with rather inaccurate values but opt to execute as many different query combinations as possible performed best in our experiments. Further, fluctuations in the measured execution times only slightly reduce the accuracy of the computed synergy values. In the optimization phase, the knowledge about synergies is then exploited by the scheduling component to minimize workload execution time. The scheduling component selects the combinations with the highest synergies to be executed next. We showed that scheduling based on synergies greatly improves workload execution times compared to a scheduling strategy according to query arrival. We further showed the effectiveness of the feedback loop during optimization. By continuously feeding monitored values back into synergy computation even after the training phase, incomplete or inaccurate synergy information is enhanced, and this results in an improved workload performance. We finally analyzed the applicability of the approach for the detection of synergies provided by database systems on the example of a commercial database system and its scan-sharing feature. In our experiments, we were able to substantiate a clear correlation between synergy values and workload execution times. We propose to transparently integrate our approach for synergy-based workload management with the company's operational database system. Our optimization component can employ arbitrary scheduling strategies, thereby offering a wide range of operation modes, from a FIFO mode with no impact at all to a synergy-based mode exploiting knowledge about positive and negative query influences on each other.

We then focused on the robust and predictable execution of single OLAP queries. In particular, we examined the join operator, which is central to OLAP query processing. When creating the execution plan for a query, the database optimizer relies on statistical and meta data to choose from a set of implemented physical join operators. Traditional join algorithms are either hash-based, sort-based, or index-based and are most appropriate when input sizes differ significantly, data is presorted, or persistent indexes are available, respectively. In case statistics are outdated or the optimization level is low, the optimizer decisions might be poor and this can lead to bad or unpredictable query performance. G-join is a new join algorithm which obviates the need for possibly wrong decisions by replacing the traditional algorithms. It combines the advantages of sort-based, hash-based, and index-based join algorithms and performs robustly in situations in which the traditional algorithms' performance decreases dramatically. G-join creates sorted runs for both inputs and then moves synchronously through the runs, while maintaining an in-memory index structure for fast probing. We showed that g-join is competitive to hash join on unsorted data and to sort-merge join on roughly sorted data. If persistent indexes exist, g-join uses them like index nested-loops join but additionally profits from the rough sort order of the probe input produced by run generation. For large unsorted inputs, g-join is more robust than hash join as it does not suffer from mistaken optimizer estimates concerning input sizes. G-join further executes the join faster than sort-merge join as it avoids the costly complete merge of sorted runs. Our hybrid g-join implementation is effective in producing first join results early and in saving I/O, and it smooths the performance decrease if the smaller input's size slightly exceeds memory. We further analyzed the impact of different design alternatives for run generation, probe index, and priority queues on performance and robustness. For run generation, replacement selection is most appropriate as it approximately halves the number of created runs compared to load-sort-store run generation algorithms. Tree-based probe indexes are more robust than hash-based indexes in the case of skewed data. For disk-bound scenarios, the performance of different priority queue implementations does not differ significantly, however, loser trees and weak-heaps minimize the number of comparison operations and are thus preferable over heaps. Besides joins, grouping operations are of great importance in OLAP processing. Query optimization faces the same risks of suboptimal decisions when choosing between traditional grouping algorithms based on sorting, hashing, or nested-loops computation. We sketched the g-aggregation algorithm, which adapts the approach of g-join for duplicate elimination and grouping, and aims at replacing traditional grouping algorithms for the sake of robustness. We propose to replace traditional join and aggregation algorithms with g-join and g-aggregation. That way, the database optimizer is relieved of the error-prone choice of physical operators, which is an important step toward robust query processing.

Finally, we turned our attention to modern hardware offering huge main memory capacities and a large number of cores. Simply porting existing algorithms to modern architectures, in particular those exhibiting non-uniform memory access (NUMA) for different main memory partitions, does not scale well. This is due to ignoring bandwidth limitations between NUMA partitions and thereby incurring expensive accesses to remote memory. We developed a suite of massively parallel sort-merge (MPSM) algorithms for the equi-join, which avoids the pitfalls of state-of-the-art algorithms on modern hardware. MPSM sorts and merge-joins chunks of data in parallel. It is designed such that no fine-grained synchronization is required between the parallel threads, thereby allowing to exploit parallelism best. The performance analysis revealed that MPSM can efficiently join very large main memory data of billions of tuples in less than three minutes. In a comparative evaluation, MPSM outperforms state-of-the-art parallel hash join proposals by factors. In particular, it outperforms the "cutting-edge" Vectorwise parallel query engine by a factor of four. Furthermore, it scales almost linearly with the number of physical cores, and even takes advantage of hyperthreading. The scalable performance of the MPSM join is due to carefully exploiting the NUMA characteristics of modern high-capacity servers. In particular, we avoided extensive (and random) accesses to remote NUMA memory partitions by including a prologue phase to redistribute the data in a way that allowed local working. Further, MPSM is based on merge join, so that it accesses remote memory only sequentially. Thereby, the remote access latency is hidden by the hardware prefetcher. While being aware of NUMA effects, MPSM is still NUMA-oblivious, i.e., not targeted at a specific NUMA architecture. In order to allow for effective use of MPSM in query processing beyond inner join computation, we engineered the MPSM for outer, semi, and anti semi joins. These variants require only little modifications to the inner join algorithm and incur almost no computational overhead. We then investigated how the roughly sorted output of MPSM can be exploited in further join processing. We found that the efficient sorting and effective use of all available cores makes the successive execution of multiple MPSM joins competitive to more elaborate techniques, which postprocess or pipeline intermediate results. Following prior approaches for hash joins, we devised MPSM teams for integrated join and aggregation processing on different keys. We propose to parallelize OLAP join processing using MPSM and thereby providing NUMA-affine and at the same time NUMA-oblivious query processing. The short response times and the scalable performance of MPSM make it applicable in operational business intelligence scenarios demanding for up-to-date strategic information.

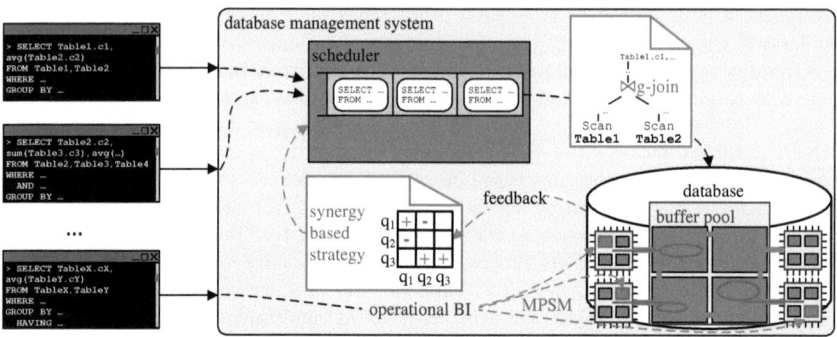

Figure 5.1: Combining the approaches for efficient, robust, and scalable OLAP query processing

We now want to give an outlook how the presented approaches can be combined to achieve the goal of efficient, robust, and scalable processing of OLAP workloads. The proposed interplay of synergy-based scheduling, robust query processing, and highly parallel in-memory query execution is sketched in Figure 5.1. Synergy-based workload management works transparently for the user and the database system and may either be realized as an independent component between the two sides or integrated into the scheduler of the database system. OLAP queries are queued and selected for execution based on their synergies with each other. The execution times are fed back to the synergy computing component in order to complete and improve the values within the synergy matrix. That way, an optimized workload execution is realized with minimal overhead. Before being executed, each single OLAP query is examined by the query optimizer to determine an efficient execution plan. Instead of relying on possibly outdated statistics to choose between a multitude of physical join operators, the optimizer employs g-join for joining two tables as g-join guarantees robust performance irrespective of input characteristics. Analogously, for aggregation and duplicate elimination, the optimizer relies on g-aggregation. The robust query execution leads to more predictable and stable execution times, which provides more useful input to synergy computation. These two techniques rather focus on robustness and the global optimization of OLAP workloads than on fast execution times of single queries. For operational business intelligence (BI) requiring "data at your fingertips" as Plattner (2009) pointed out, additional available resources like buffer pool frames or processing cores are effectively used by MPSM, providing join performance which scales linearly with the offered level of parallelism.

Bibliography

AHMAD, M., ABOULNAGA, A., BABU, S., AND MUNAGALA, K.: Modeling and Exploiting Query Interactions in Database Systems. In: *Proceedings of the ACM 17th International Conference on Information and Knowledge Management (CIKM)*, Napa, California, USA, 2008.

ALBUTIU, M.-C. AND KEMPER, A.: Synergy-based Workload Management. In: RIGAUX, P. AND SENELLART, P. (eds.), *Proceedings of the VLDB PhD Workshop*, VLDB Endowment, 2009.

ALBUTIU, M.-C., KEMPER, A., AND NEUMANN, T.: Massively Parallel Sort-Merge Joins in Main Memory Multi-Core Database Systems. *Proceedings of the VLDB Endowment (PVLDB)*, 5(10):1064–1075, 2012a.

ALBUTIU, M.-C., KEMPER, A., AND NEUMANN, T.: Massively Parallel Sort-Merge Joins in Main Memory Multi-Core Database Systems. *CoRR*, abs/1207.0145, 2012b.

ALBUTIU, M.-C., KEMPER, A., AND NEUMANN, T.: Extending the MPSM Join. In: MARKL, V., SAAKE, G., SATTLER, K.-U., HACKENBROICH, G., MITSCHANG, B., HÄRDER, T., AND KÖPPEN, V. (eds.), *BTW*, LNI, pp. 57–71, GI, 2013, ISBN 978-3-88579-608-4.

ALBUTIU, M.-C., SCHOLZ, A., KROMPASS, S., AND KEMPER, A.: Synergie-basiertes Scheduling von Datenbank-Workloads. *Datenbank-Spektrum*, 8(28):44–51, 2009.

BITTON, D. AND DEWITT, D. J.: Duplicate Record Elimination in Large Data Files. *ACM Transactions on Database Systems (TODS)*, 8(2):255–265, 1983.

BLANAS, S., LI, Y., AND PATEL, J. M.: Design and Evaluation of Main Memory Hash Join Algorithms for Multi-core CPUs. In: *Proceedings of the ACM SIGMOD International Conference on Management of Data*, pp. 37–48, 2011.

BLANAS, S. AND PATEL, J. M.: How efficient is our radix join implementation? http://pages.cs.wisc.edu/~sblanas/files/comparison.pdf, 2011.

BONCZ, P. A., MANEGOLD, S., AND KERSTEN, M. L.: Database Architecture Optimized for the New Bottleneck: Memory Access. In: *Proceedings of the 25th International Conference on Very Large Data Bases (VLDB)*, pp. 54–65, 1999.

BONCZ, P. A., MANEGOLD, S., AND KERSTEN, M. L.: Database Architecture Evolution: Mammals Flourished long before Dinosaurs became Extinct. *Proceedings of the VLDB Endowment (PVLDB)*, 2(2):1648–1653, 2009.

CHEN, S., AILAMAKI, A., GIBBONS, P. B., AND MOWRY, T. C.: Improving Hash Join Performance Through Prefetching. *ACM Transactions on Database Systems (TODS)*, 32(3):17, 2007.

CHHUGANI, J., NGUYEN, A. D., LEE, V. W., MACY, W., HAGOG, M., CHEN, Y.-K., BARANSI, A., KUMAR, S., AND DUBEY, P.: Efficient Implementation of Sorting on Multi-Core SIMD CPU Architecture. *Proceedings of the VLDB Endowment (PVLDB)*, 1(2):1313–1324, 2008.

CHOENNI, S., KERSTEN, M. L., AND VAN DEN AKKER, J. F. P.: A Framework for Multi Query Optimization. In: *Proceedings of the 8th International Conference on Management of Data (COMAD)*, pp. 165–182, Madras, India, 1997.

CIESLEWICZ, J. AND ROSS, K. A.: Data partitioning on chip multiprocessors. In: *Proceedings of the 4th International Workshop on Data Management on New Hardware (DaMoN)*, pp. 25–34, 2008.

CLAUSSEN, J., KEMPER, A., KOSSMANN, D., AND WIESNER, C.: Exploiting Early Sorting and Early Partitioning for Decision Support Query Processing. *The VLDB Journal*, 9(3):190–213, 2000.

DALVI, N. N., SANGHAI, S. K., ROY, P., AND SUDARSHAN, S.: Pipelining in multiquery optimization. *Journal of Computer and System Sciences*, 66(4):728–762, 2003.

DEAN, J. AND GHEMAWAT, S.: MapReduce: Simplified Data Processing on Large Clusters. In: *Proceedings of the 6th Symposium on Operating Systems Design and Implementation (OSDI)*, pp. 137–150, 2004.

DEWITT, D. J., GHANDEHARIZADEH, S., SCHNEIDER, D. A., BRICKER, A., HSIAO, H.-I., AND RASMUSSEN, R.: The Gamma Database Machine Project. *IEEE Transactions on Knowledge and Data Engineering*, 2(1):44–62, 1990.

DEWITT, D. J., KATZ, R. H., OLKEN, F., SHAPIRO, L. D., STONEBRAKER, M., AND WOOD, D. A.: Implementation Techniques for Main Memory Database Systems. In: YORMARK, B. (ed.), *Proceedings of the ACM SIGMOD International Conference on Management of Data*, pp. 1–8, ACM Press, 1984.

DEWITT, D. J., NAUGHTON, J. F., AND BURGER, J.: Nested Loops Revisited. In: *Proceedings of the 2nd International Conference on Parallel and Distributed Information Systems (PDIS)*, pp. 230–242, 1993.

DEWITT, D. J., NAUGHTON, J. F., SCHNEIDER, D. A., AND SESHADRI, S.: Practical Skew Handling in Parallel Joins. In: *Proceedings of the 18th International Conference on Very Large Data Bases (VLDB)*, pp. 27–40, 1992.

DITTRICH, J.-P., SEEGER, B., TAYLOR, D. S., AND WIDMAYER, P.: Progressive Merge Join: A Generic and Non-blocking Sort-based Join Algorithm. In: *Proceedings of the 28th International Conference on Very Large Data Bases (VLDB)*, pp. 299–310, 2002.

DUTTON, R. D.: The weak-heap data structure. Technical Report CS-TR-92-09, Department of Computer Science, University of Central Florida, Orlando, FL 32816, 1992.

DUTTON, R. D.: Weak-Heap Sort. *BIT Numerical Mathematics*, 33(3):372–381, 1993.

EDELKAMP, S. AND WEGENER, I.: On the Performance of WEAK-HEAPSORT. In: *STACS*, pp. 254–266, 2000.

FÄRBER, F., CHA, S. K., PRIMSCH, J., BORNHÖVD, C., SIGG, S., AND LEHNER, W.: SAP HANA Database: Data Management for Modern Business Applications. *SIGMOD Record*, 40(4):45–51, 2011, ISSN 0163-5808.

FREY, P. W., GONCALVES, R., KERSTEN, M., AND TEUBNER, J.: Spinning Relations: High-speed Networks for Distributed Join Processing. In: *Proceedings of the 5th International Workshop on Data Management on New Hardware (DaMoN)*, pp. 27–33, 2009, ISBN 978-1-60558-701-1.

FUSHIMI, S., KITSUREGAWA, M., AND TANAKA, H.: An Overview of The System Software of A Parallel Relational Database Machine GRACE. In: *Proceedings of the 12th International Conference on Very Large Data Bases (VLDB)*, pp. 209–219, 1986.

GARCIA, L. C., LINDQUIST, D. B., AND ROLLO, G. F.: Sorting/Merging Tree for Determining a next Tournament Champion in each Cycle by Simultaneously Comparing Records in a Path of the Previous Tournament Champion. February 1994.

GRAEFE, G.: Query Evaluation Techniques for Large Databases. *ACM Comput. Surv.*, 25(2):73–170, 1993.

GRAEFE, G.: Sort-Merge-Join: An Idea Whose Time Has(h) Passed? In: *Proceedings of the 10th International Conference on Data Engineering (ICDE)*, pp. 406–417, 1994.

GRAEFE, G.: A Generalized Join Algorithm. In: *Proceedings of the 14th German Conference on Database Systems for Business, Technology and Web (BTW)*, pp. 267–286, 2011.

GRAEFE, G.: New Algorithms for Join and Grouping Operations. *Computer Science - Research&Development*, 27(1):3–27, 2012.

GRAEFE, G., BUNKER, R., AND COOPER, S.: Hash Joins and Hash Teams in Microsoft SQL Server. In: *Proceedings of the 24th International Conference on Very Large Data Bases (VLDB)*, pp. 86–97, 1998.

GRAEFE, G. AND LARSON, P.-Å.: B-Tree Indexes and CPU Caches. In: *Proceedings of the 17th International Conference on Data Engineering (ICDE)*, pp. 349–358, 2001.

HE, B., YANG, K., FANG, R., LU, M., GOVINDARAJU, N. K., LUO, Q., AND SANDER, P. V.: Relational Joins on Graphics Processors. In: *Proceedings of the ACM SIGMOD International Conference on Management of Data*, pp. 511–524, 2008.

HELMER, S., WESTMANN, T., AND MOERKOTTE, G.: Diag-Join: An Opportunistic Join Algorithm for 1:N Relationships. In: *Proceedings of the 24th International Conference on Very Large Data Bases (VLDB)*, pp. 98–109, 1998.

HP: HP NeoView Workload Management Services Guide. August 2007.

INKSTER, D., ZUKOWSKI, M., AND BONCZ, P.: Integration of VectorWise with Ingres. *SIGMOD Record*, 40:45–53, November 2011, ISSN 0163-5808.

KEMPER, A., KOSSMANN, D., AND WIESNER, C.: Generalized Hash Teams for Join and Group-by. In: *Proceedings of the 25th International Conference on Very Large Data Bases (VLDB)*, pp. 30–41, 1999.

KEMPER, A. AND NEUMANN, T.: HyPer: A Hybrid OLTP&OLAP Main Memory Database System Based on Virtual Memory Snapshots. In: *Proceedings of the 27th International Conference on Data Engineering (ICDE)*, pp. 195–206, 2011.

KIM, C., SEDLAR, E., CHHUGANI, J., KALDEWEY, T., NGUYEN, A. D., BLAS, A. D., LEE, V. W., SATISH, N., AND DUBEY, P.: Sort vs. Hash Revisited: Fast Join Implementation on Modern Multi-Core CPUs. *Proceedings of the VLDB Endowment (PVLDB)*, 2(2):1378–1389, 2009.

KITSUREGAWA, M., TANAKA, H., AND MOTO-OKA, T.: Application of Hash to Data Base Machine and Its Architecture. *New Generation Computing*, 1(1):63–74, 1983.

KNUTH, D. E.: *The Art of Computer Programming, Vol. III: Sorting and Searching*. Addison-Wesley, 1973, ISBN 0-201-03803-X.

KROMPASS, S., SCHOLZ, A., ALBUTIU, M.-C., KUNO, H. A., WIENER, J. L., DAYAL, U., AND KEMPER, A.: Quality of Service-enabled Management of Database Workloads. *IEEE Data Eng. Bull.*, 31(1):20–27, 2008.

LANG, C. A., BHATTACHARJEE, B., MALKEMUS, T., AND WONG, K.: Increasing Buffer-Locality for Multiple Index Based Scans through Intelligent Placement and Index Scan Speed Control. In: *Proceedings of the 33rd International Conference on Very Large Data Bases (VLDB)*, pp. 1298–1309, 2007.

LARSON, P.-Å.: External Sorting: Run Formation Revisited. *IEEE Transactions on Knowledge and Data Engineering*, 15(4):961–972, 2003.

LARSON, P.-Å. AND GRAEFE, G.: Memory Management During Run Generation in External Sorting. In: *Proceedings of the ACM SIGMOD International Conference on Management of Data*, pp. 472–483, 1998.

LEE, R., ZHOU, M., AND LIAO, H.: Request Window: an Approach to Improve Throughput of RDBMS-based Data Integration System by Utilizing Data Sharing Across Concurrent Distributed Queries. In: *Proceedings of the 33rd International Conference on Very Large Data Bases (VLDB)*, pp. 1219–1230, 2007.

LI, G.: *On the Design and Evaluation of a New Order-Based Join Algorithm*. Master's Thesis, University of California, Irvine, 2010.

LOMET, D. B.: The Evolution of Effective B-tree Page Organization and Techniques: A Personal Account. *SIGMOD Record*, 30(3):64–69, 2001.

MANEGOLD, S., BONCZ, P. A., AND KERSTEN, M. L.: Optimizing Main-Memory Join on Modern Hardware. *IEEE Transactions on Knowledge and Data Engineering*, 14(4):709–730, 2002.

MARKL, V., HAAS, P. J., KUTSCH, M., MEGIDDO, N., SRIVASTAVA, U., AND TRAN, T. M.: Consistent Selectivity Estimation via Maximum Entropy. *The VLDB Journal*, 16(1):55–76, 2007, ISSN 1066-8888.

MARTINEZ-PALAU, X., DOMINGUEZ-SAL, D., AND LARRIBA-PEY, J.-L.: Two-way Replacement Selection. *Proceedings of the VLDB Endowment (PVLDB)*, 3(1):871–881, 2010.

Microsoft: Microsoft SQL Server 2005 Books Online. http://msdn2.microsoft.com/en-us/library/ms190419.aspx, September 2007.

NEUMANN, T.: Efficiently Compiling Efficient Query Plans for Modern Hardware. In: *Proceedings of the 37th International Conference on Very Large Data Bases (VLDB)*, 2011.

NIU, B., MARTIN, P., POWLEY, W., HORMAN, R., AND BIRD, P.: Workload Adaptation In Autonomic DBMSs. In: *Proceedings of the 16th International Conference of the Center for Advanced Studies on Collaborative Research (CASCON)*, 2006.

O'GORMAN, K., AGRAWAL, D., AND ABBADI, A. E.: Multiple Query Optimization by Cache-Aware Middleware Using Query Teamwork. In: *Proceedings of the 18th International Conference on Data Engineering (ICDE)*, p. 274, 2002.

Oracle: The Oracle Database Resource Manager: Scheduling CPU Resources at the Application Level. http://research.microsoft.com/~jamesrh/hpts2001/submissions/, 2001.

OTT, D. E.: Optimizing Software Applications for NUMA, Intel Whitepaper. http://software.intel.com/en-us/articles/optimizing-software-applications-for-numa/, 2009.

PLATTNER, H.: A common database approach for OLTP and OLAP using an in-memory column database. In: *Proceedings of the ACM SIGMOD International Conference on Management of Data*, pp. 1–2, 2009.

RAMAKRISHNAN, R. AND GEHRKE, J.: *Database Management Systems (3. ed.)*. McGraw-Hill, 2003, ISBN 978-0-07-115110-8.

REDDY, N. AND HARITSA, J. R.: Analyzing Plan Diagrams of Database Query Optimizers. In: *Proceedings of the 31st International Conference on Very Large Data Bases (VLDB)*, pp. 1228–1239, 2005, ISBN 1-59593-154-6.

Ross, K. A. AND CIESLEWICZ, J.: Optimal Splitters for Database Partitioning with Size Bounds. In: *Proceedings of the 12th International Conference on Database Theory (ICDT)*, pp. 98–110, 2009.

Roy, P., SESHADRI, S., SUDARSHAN, S., AND BHOBE, S.: Efficient and Extensible Algorithms for Multi Query Optimization. In: *Proceedings of the ACM SIGMOD International Conference on Management of Data*, pp. 249–260, 2000.

SCHROEDER, B., HARCHOL-BALTER, M., IYENGAR, A., NAHUM, E., AND WIERMAN, A.: How to Determine a Good Multi-Programming Level for External Scheduling. In: *Proceedings of the 22nd International Conference on Data Engineering (ICDE)*, p. 60, 2006, ISBN 0-7695-2570-9.

SELINGER, P. G., ASTRAHAN, M. M., CHAMBERLIN, D. D., LORIE, R. A., AND PRICE, T. G.: Access Path Selection in a Relational Database Management System. In: *Proceedings of the ACM SIGMOD International Conference on Management of Data*, pp. 23–34, 1979.

SUBRAMANIAN, N. AND VENKATARAMAN, S.: Cost Based Optimization of Decision Support Queries using Transient-Views. In: *Proceedings of the ACM SIGMOD International Conference on Management of Data*, pp. 319–330, June 1998.

TEUBNER, J. AND MÜLLER, R.: How soccer players would do stream joins. In: *Proceedings of the ACM SIGMOD International Conference on Management of Data*, pp. 625–636, 2011.

TPC-C: TPC Benchmark C. http://www.tpc.org/tpcc.

TPC-H: TPC Benchmark H (Decision Support). http://www.tpc.org/tpch.

VOLTDB LLC: VoltDB Technical Overview, Whitepaper. 2010.

WYLEZICH, G.: *Evaluierung verschiedener Testumgebungen für den Einsatz von Synergie-basiertem Scheduling*. Master's Thesis, Technische Universität München, 2011.

YAN, W. P. AND LARSON, P.-Å.: Data Reduction Through Early Grouping. In: *Proceedings of the 4th International Conference of the Center for Advanced Studies on Collaborative Research (CASCON)*, p. 74, 1994.

ZUKOWSKI, M., HÉMAN, S., NES, N., AND BONCZ, P. A.: Cooperative Scans: Dynamic Bandwidth Sharing in a DBMS. In: *Proceedings of the 33rd International Conference on Very Large Data Bases (VLDB)*, pp. 723–734, 2007.

i want morebooks!

Buy your books fast and straightforward online - at one of world's fastest growing online book stores! Environmentally sound due to Print-on-Demand technologies.

Buy your books online at
www.get-morebooks.com

Kaufen Sie Ihre Bücher schnell und unkompliziert online – auf einer der am schnellsten wachsenden Buchhandelsplattformen weltweit! Dank Print-On-Demand umwelt- und ressourcenschonend produziert.

Bücher schneller online kaufen
www.morebooks.de

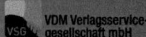

VDM Verlagsservicegesellschaft mbH
Heinrich-Böcking-Str. 6-8 Telefon: +49 681 3720 174 info@vdm-vsg.de
D - 66121 Saarbrücken Telefax: +49 681 3720 1749 www.vdm-vsg.de

Printed by Books on Demand GmbH, Norderstedt / Germany